WILLIAM TELL

ONE AGAINST AN EMPIRE

A
SWISS
LEGEND

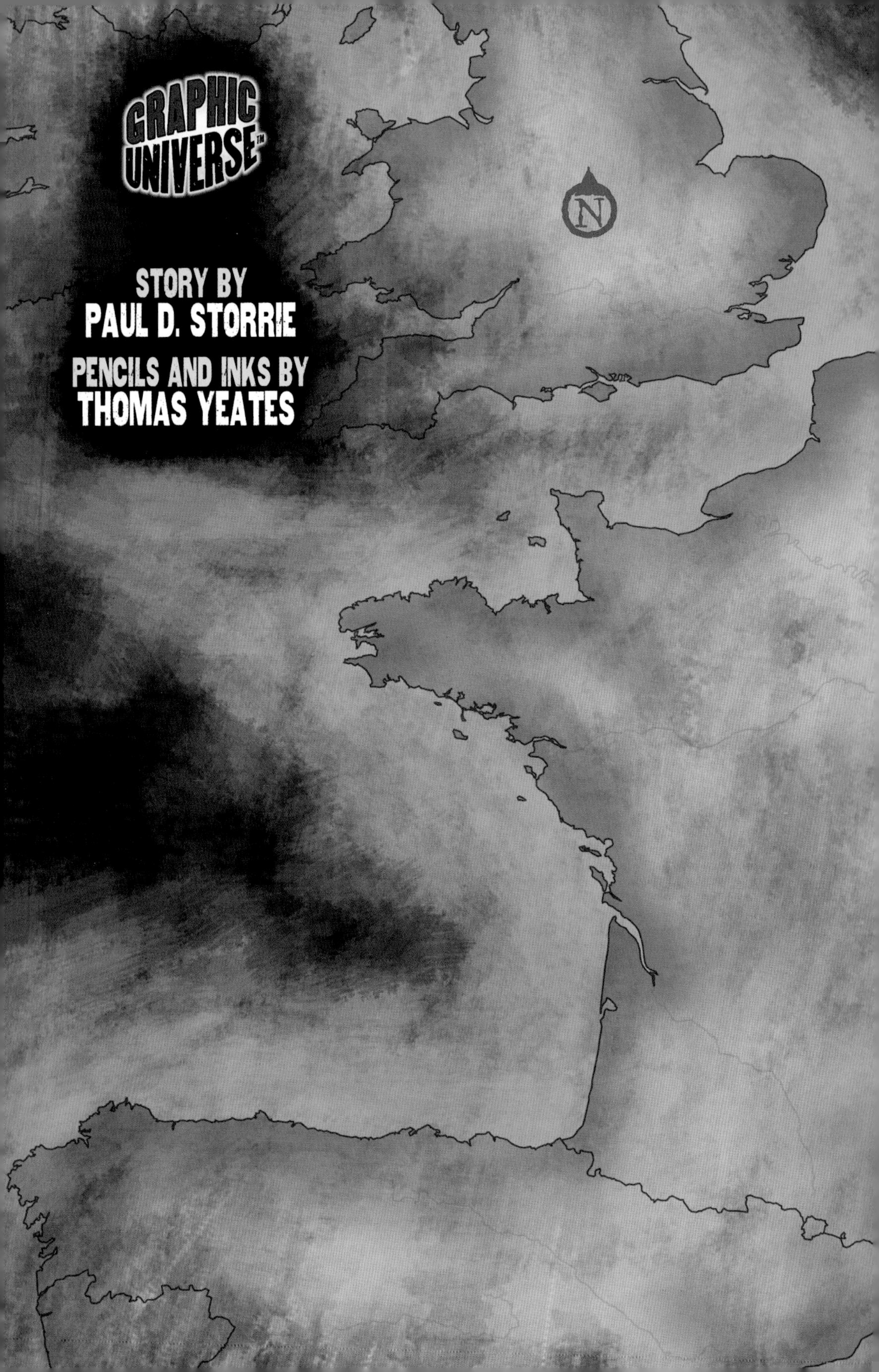
N

GRAPHIC UNIVERSE™

STORY BY
PAUL D. STORRIE
PENCILS AND INKS BY
THOMAS YEATES

WILLIAM TELL

ONE AGAINST AN EMPIRE

A SWISS LEGEND

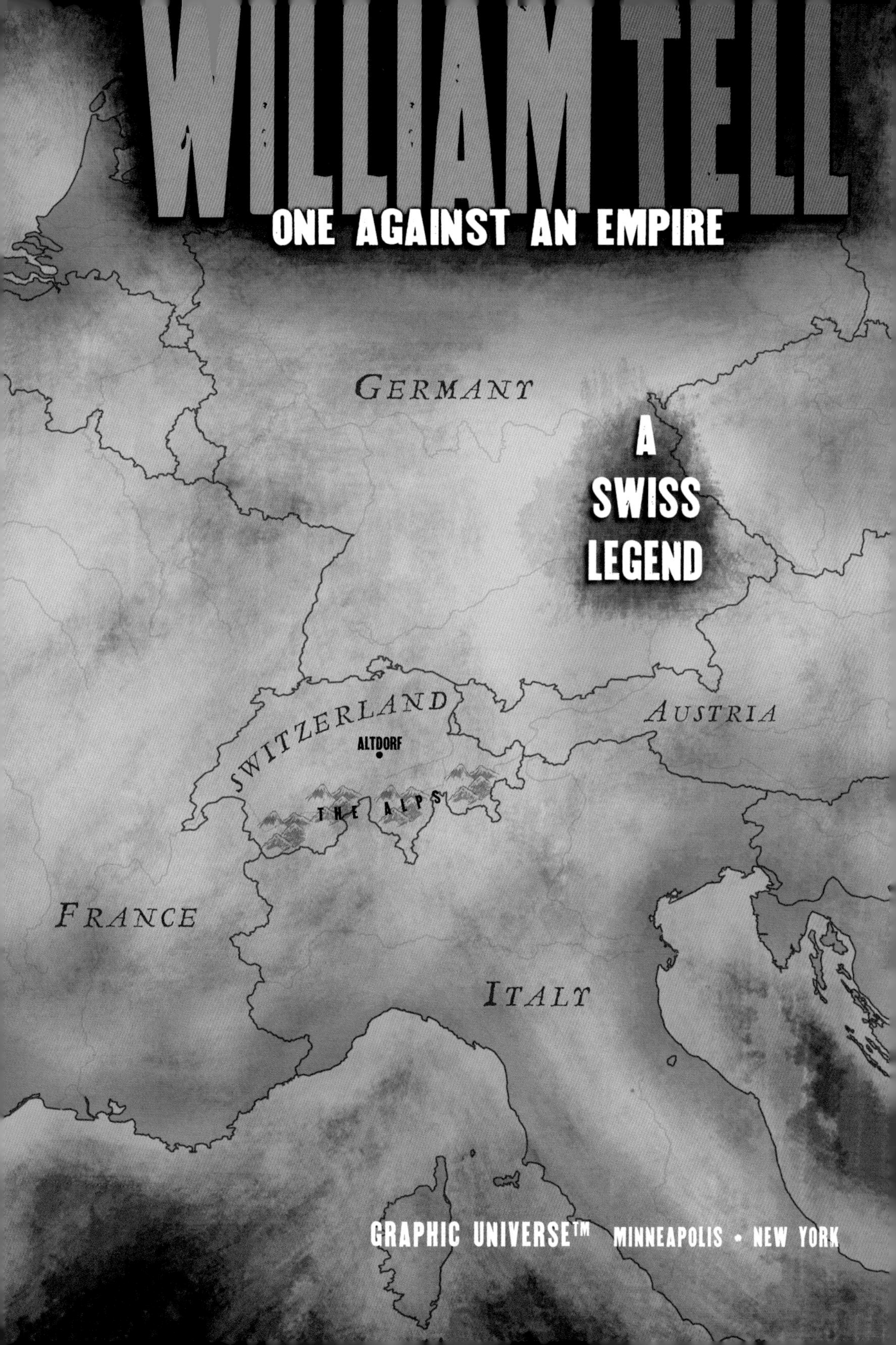
GERMANY
AUSTRIA
SWITZERLAND
ALTDORF
THE ALPS
FRANCE
ITALY

GRAPHIC UNIVERSE™ MINNEAPOLIS • NEW YORK

WILLIAM TELL MAY OR MAY NOT HAVE BEEN AN ACTUAL PERSON. REAL OR NOT, THE STORY OF HIS BRAVE DEEDS HAS BECOME A VITAL PART OF SWISS HISTORY. TO WRITE THIS EXCITING GRAPHIC NOVEL, AUTHOR PAUL D. STORRIE REFERRED TO THE BEST-KNOWN AND MOST RESPECTED SOURCES OF THE TELL LEGEND—THE PLAY WILHELM TELL (1804) BY GERMAN WRITER FRIEDRICH SCHILLER, AND WILLIAM TELL TOLD AGAIN (1904) BY THE ENGLISH WRITER P. G. WODEHOUSE. ARTIST THOMAS YEATES STUDIED BOTH MEDIEVAL AND MODERN SOURCES TO CREATE THE AUTHENTIC DRESS AND SETTING OF THE STORY.

STORY BY PAUL D. STORRIE

PENCILS AND INKS BY THOMAS YEATES
WITH SPECIAL THANKS TO NIKI

COLORING BY HI-FI DESIGN

LETTERING BY MARSHALL DILLON AND
TERRI DELGADO

CONSULTANT: THERESA KRIER, PH.D.,
MACALESTER COLLEGE

Copyright © 2009 by Lerner Publishing Group, Inc.

Graphic Universe™ is a trademark of Lerner Publishing Group, Inc.

Graphic Universe™
A division of Lerner Publishing Group, Inc.
241 First Avenue North
Minneapolis, MN 55401 U.S.A.

Website: www.lernerbooks.com

Library of Congress Cataloging-in-Publication Data

Storrie, Paul D.
    William Tell : one against an empire / story by Paul D. Storrie ; pencils and inks by Thomas Yeates.
       p.   cm. — (Graphic myths and legends)
    Includes index.
    ISBN: 978-0-8225-7175-9 (lib. bdg. : alk. paper)
       1. Tell, Wilhelm—Comic books, strips, etc.
    2. Graphic novels. I. Yeates, Thomas. II. Title.
    DQ92.S76 2009
    949.4'01—dc22   2007038657

Manufactured in the United States of America
1 2 3 4 5 6 - DP - 14 13 12 11 10 09

TABLE OF CONTENTS

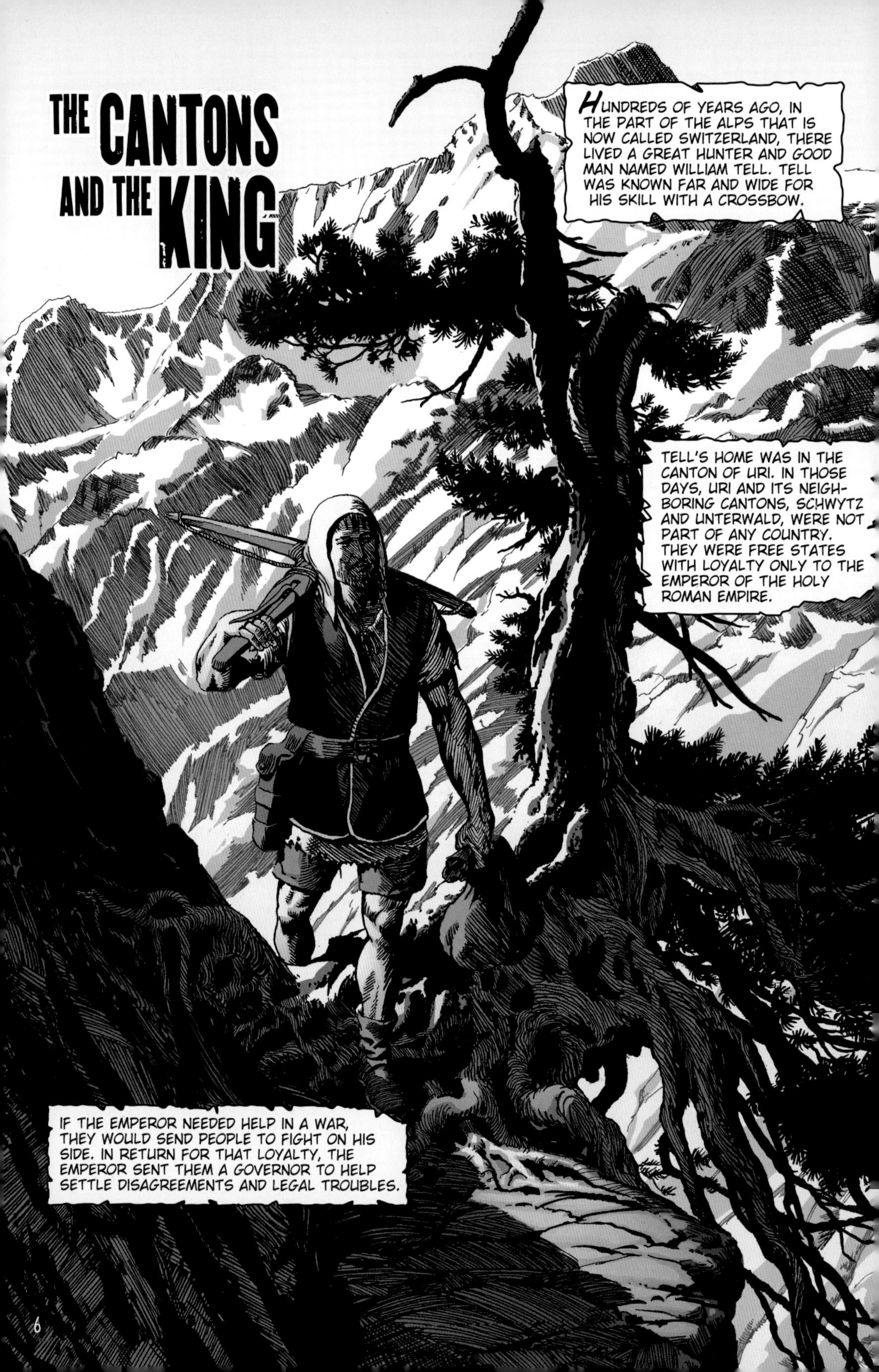
THE CANTONS AND THE KING
HUNDREDS OF YEARS AGO, IN THE PART OF THE ALPS THAT IS NOW CALLED SWITZERLAND, THERE LIVED A GREAT HUNTER AND GOOD MAN NAMED WILLIAM TELL. TELL WAS KNOWN FAR AND WIDE FOR HIS SKILL WITH A CROSSBOW.
TELL'S HOME WAS IN THE CANTON OF URI. IN THOSE DAYS, URI AND ITS NEIGH-BORING CANTONS, SCHWYTZ AND UNTERWALD, WERE NOT PART OF ANY COUNTRY. THEY WERE FREE STATES WITH LOYALTY ONLY TO THE EMPEROR OF THE HOLY ROMAN EMPIRE.
IF THE EMPEROR NEEDED HELP IN A WAR, THEY WOULD SEND PEOPLE TO FIGHT ON HIS SIDE. IN RETURN FOR THAT LOYALTY, THE EMPEROR SENT THEM A GOVERNOR TO HELP SETTLE DISAGREEMENTS AND LEGAL TROUBLES.

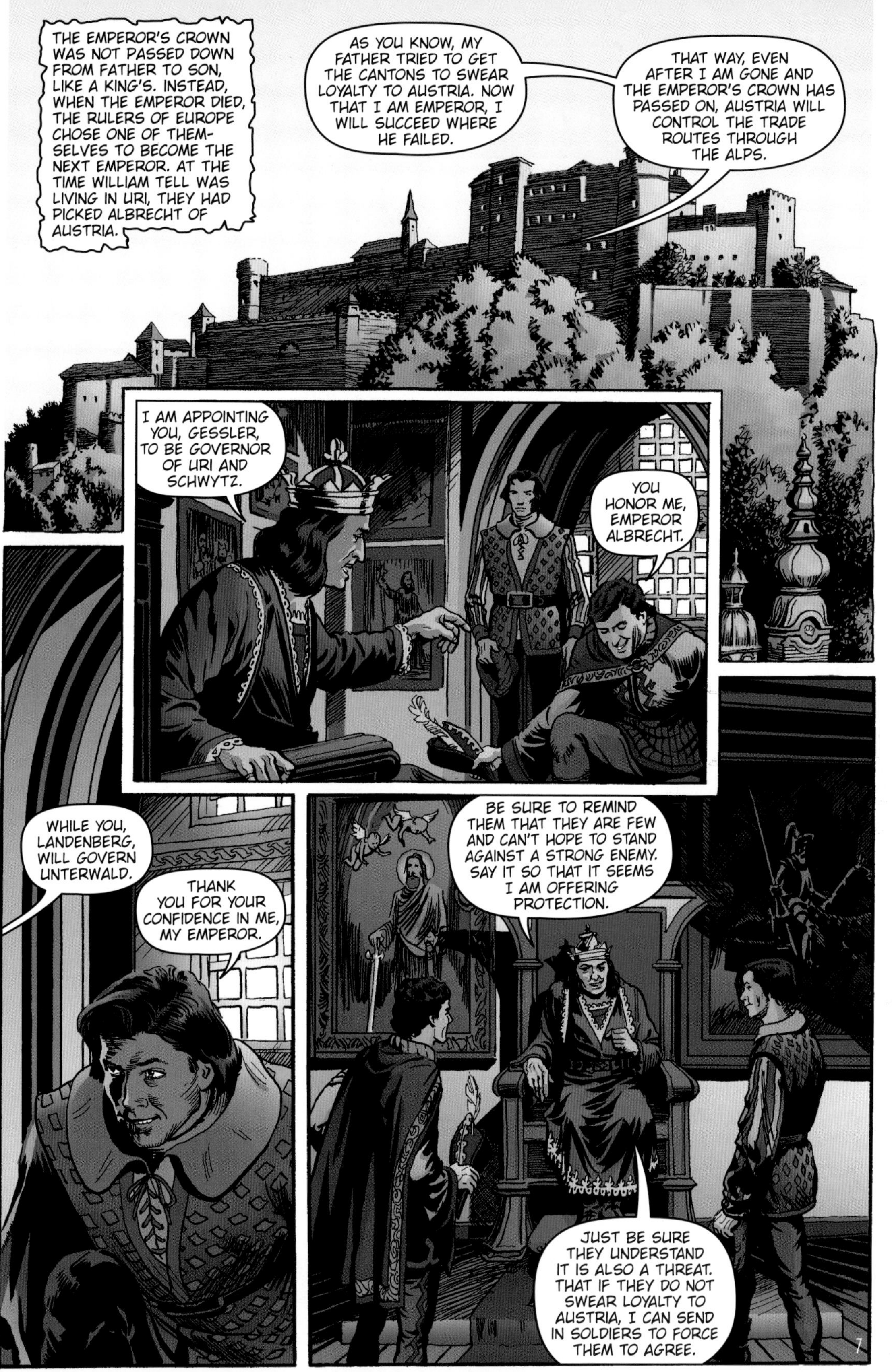
THE EMPEROR'S CROWN WAS NOT PASSED DOWN FROM FATHER TO SON, LIKE A KING'S. INSTEAD, WHEN THE EMPEROR DIED, THE RULERS OF EUROPE CHOSE ONE OF THEMSELVES TO BECOME THE NEXT EMPEROR. AT THE TIME WILLIAM TELL WAS LIVING IN URI, THEY HAD PICKED ALBRECHT OF AUSTRIA.
AS YOU KNOW, MY FATHER TRIED TO GET THE CANTONS TO SWEAR LOYALTY TO AUSTRIA. NOW THAT I AM EMPEROR, I WILL SUCCEED WHERE HE FAILED.
THAT WAY, EVEN AFTER I AM GONE AND THE EMPEROR'S CROWN HAS PASSED ON, AUSTRIA WILL CONTROL THE TRADE ROUTES THROUGH THE ALPS.
I AM APPOINTING YOU, GESSLER, TO BE GOVERNOR OF URI AND SCHWYTZ.
YOU HONOR ME, EMPEROR ALBRECHT.
WHILE YOU, LANDENBERG, WILL GOVERN UNTERWALD.
THANK YOU FOR YOUR CONFIDENCE IN ME, MY EMPEROR.
BE SURE TO REMIND THEM THAT THEY ARE FEW AND CAN'T HOPE TO STAND AGAINST A STRONG ENEMY. SAY IT SO THAT IT SEEMS I AM OFFERING PROTECTION.
JUST BE SURE THEY UNDERSTAND IT IS ALSO A THREAT. THAT IF THEY DO NOT SWEAR LOYALTY TO AUSTRIA, I CAN SEND IN SOLDIERS TO FORCE THEM TO AGREE.

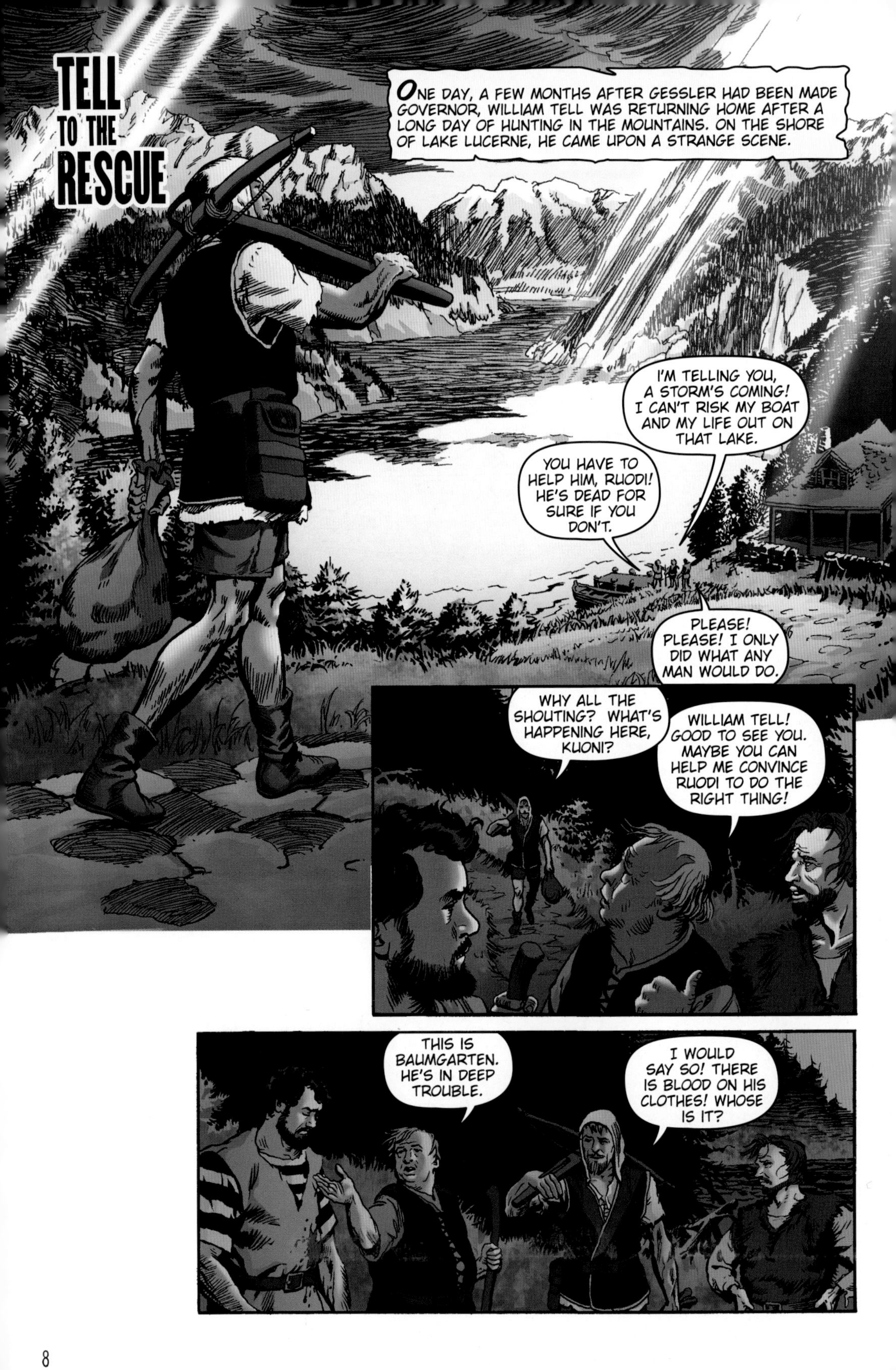
TELL TO THE RESCUE
ONE DAY, A FEW MONTHS AFTER GESSLER HAD BEEN MADE GOVERNOR, WILLIAM TELL WAS RETURNING HOME AFTER A LONG DAY OF HUNTING IN THE MOUNTAINS. ON THE SHORE OF LAKE LUCERNE, HE CAME UPON A STRANGE SCENE.
YOU HAVE TO HELP HIM, RUODI! HE'S DEAD FOR SURE IF YOU DON'T.
I'M TELLING YOU, A STORM'S COMING! I CAN'T RISK MY BOAT AND MY LIFE OUT ON THAT LAKE.
PLEASE! PLEASE! I ONLY DID WHAT ANY MAN WOULD DO.
WHY ALL THE SHOUTING? WHAT'S HAPPENING HERE, KUONI?
WILLIAM TELL! GOOD TO SEE YOU. MAYBE YOU CAN HELP ME CONVINCE RUODI TO DO THE RIGHT THING!
THIS IS BAUMGARTEN. HE'S IN DEEP TROUBLE.
I WOULD SAY SO! THERE IS BLOOD ON HIS CLOTHES! WHOSE IS IT?

I WILL NOT LIE. IT BELONGS TO THE SENESCHAL OF CASTLE ROSSBERG. I HAVE KILLED HIM.

YOU KILLED THE CASTLE'S KEEPER? WHY ON EARTH WOULD YOU DO SUCH A THING?

FOR THE BEST OF REASONS. TO PROTECT MY WIFE! HE ATTACKED HER WHILE I WAS IN THE FOREST GATHERING WOOD. I CAME HOME JUST IN TIME.

I TOOK MY AXE AND FELLED HIM LIKE A TREE! ANY MAN WOULD HAVE DONE THE SAME!

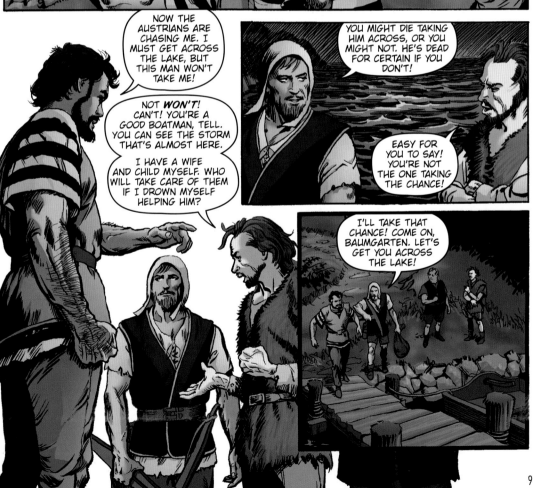

NOW THE AUSTRIANS ARE CHASING ME. I MUST GET ACROSS THE LAKE, BUT THIS MAN WON'T TAKE ME!

YOU MIGHT DIE TAKING HIM ACROSS, OR YOU MIGHT NOT. HE'S DEAD FOR CERTAIN IF YOU DON'T!

NOT *WON'T*! CAN'T! YOU'RE A GOOD BOATMAN, TELL. YOU CAN SEE THE STORM THAT'S ALMOST HERE.

I HAVE A WIFE AND CHILD MYSELF. WHO WILL TAKE CARE OF THEM IF I DROWN MYSELF HELPING HIM?

EASY FOR YOU TO SAY! YOU'RE NOT THE ONE TAKING THE CHANCE!

I'LL TAKE THAT CHANCE! COME ON, BAUMGARTEN. LET'S GET YOU ACROSS THE LAKE!

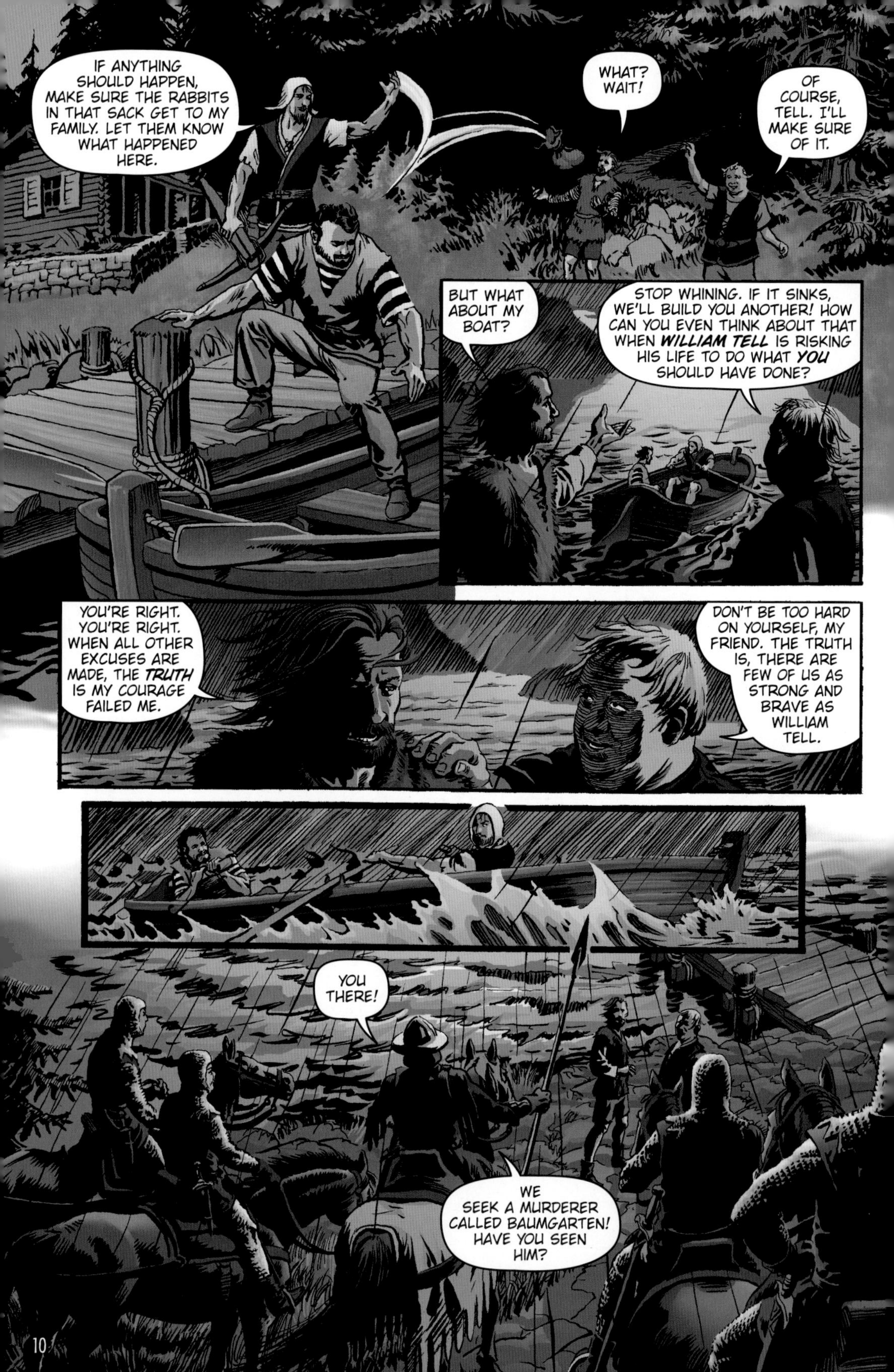
IF ANYTHING SHOULD HAPPEN, MAKE SURE THE RABBITS IN THAT SACK GET TO MY FAMILY. LET THEM KNOW WHAT HAPPENED HERE.
WHAT? WAIT!
OF COURSE, TELL. I'LL MAKE SURE OF IT.
BUT WHAT ABOUT MY BOAT?
STOP WHINING. IF IT SINKS, WE'LL BUILD YOU ANOTHER! HOW CAN YOU EVEN THINK ABOUT THAT WHEN WILLIAM TELL IS RISKING HIS LIFE TO DO WHAT YOU SHOULD HAVE DONE?
YOU'RE RIGHT. YOU'RE RIGHT. WHEN ALL OTHER EXCUSES ARE MADE, THE TRUTH IS MY COURAGE FAILED ME.
DON'T BE TOO HARD ON YOURSELF, MY FRIEND. THE TRUTH IS, THERE ARE FEW OF US AS STRONG AND BRAVE AS WILLIAM TELL.
YOU THERE!
WE SEEK A MURDERER CALLED BAUMGARTEN! HAVE YOU SEEN HIM?

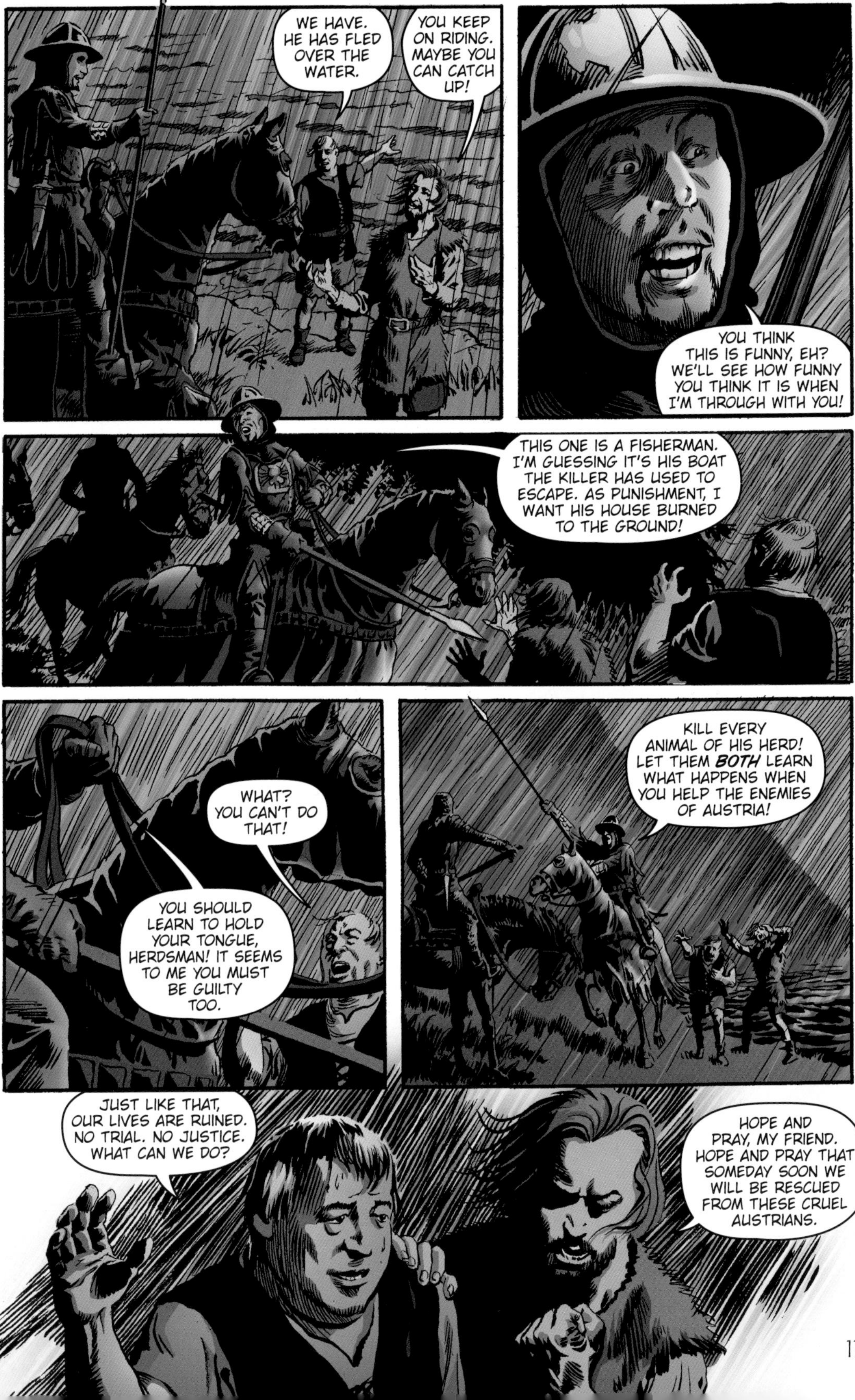
WE HAVE. HE HAS FLED OVER THE WATER.
YOU KEEP ON RIDING. MAYBE YOU CAN CATCH UP!
YOU THINK THIS IS FUNNY, EH? WE'LL SEE HOW FUNNY YOU THINK IT IS WHEN I'M THROUGH WITH YOU!
THIS ONE IS A FISHERMAN. I'M GUESSING IT'S HIS BOAT THE KILLER HAS USED TO ESCAPE. AS PUNISHMENT, I WANT HIS HOUSE BURNED TO THE GROUND!
WHAT? YOU CAN'T DO THAT!
YOU SHOULD LEARN TO HOLD YOUR TONGUE, HERDSMAN! IT SEEMS TO ME YOU MUST BE GUILTY TOO.
KILL EVERY ANIMAL OF HIS HERD! LET THEM BOTH LEARN WHAT HAPPENS WHEN YOU HELP THE ENEMIES OF AUSTRIA!
JUST LIKE THAT, OUR LIVES ARE RUINED. NO TRIAL. NO JUSTICE. WHAT CAN WE DO?
HOPE AND PRAY, MY FRIEND. HOPE AND PRAY THAT SOMEDAY SOON WE WILL BE RESCUED FROM THESE CRUEL AUSTRIANS.

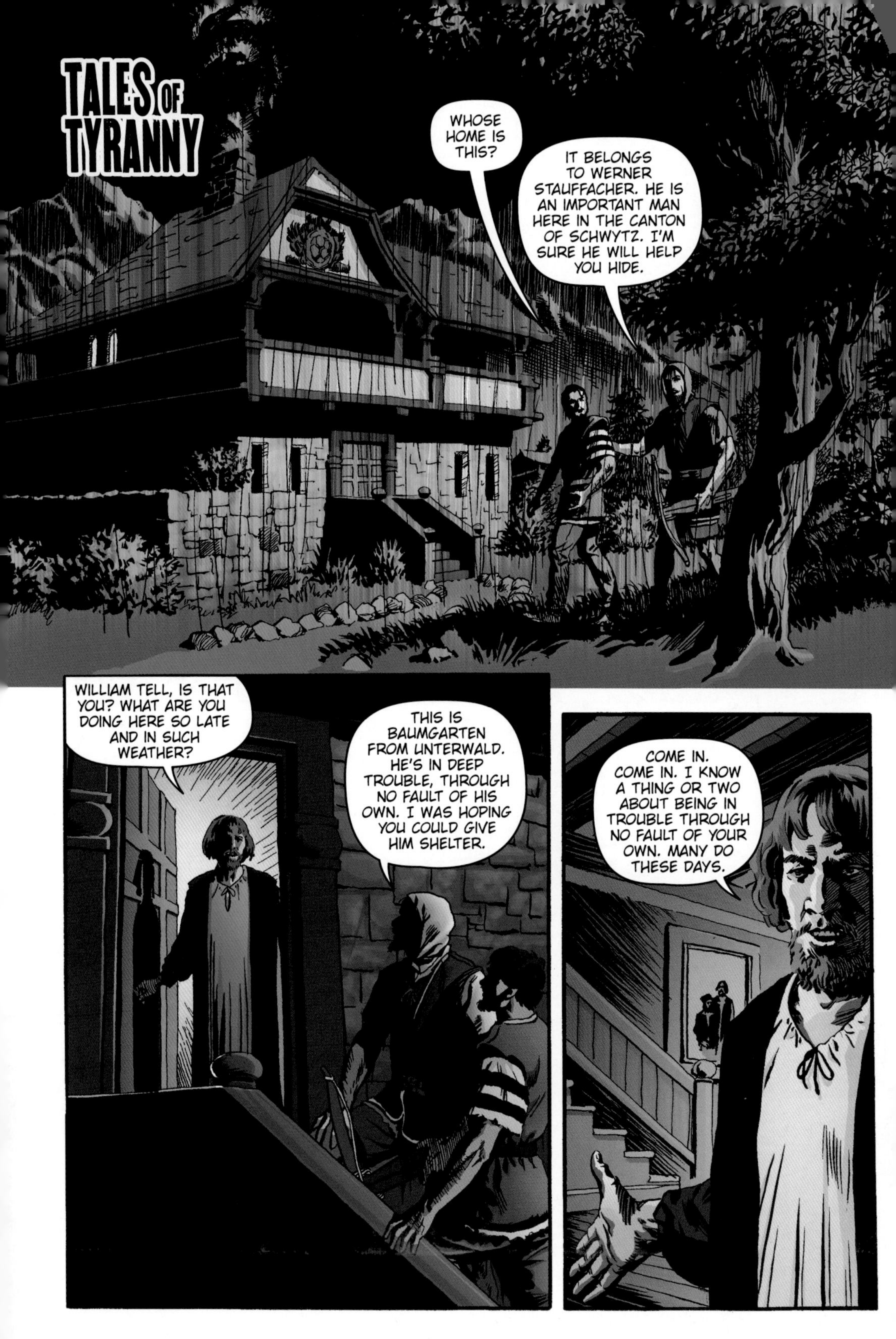
TALES OF TYRANNY
WHOSE HOME IS THIS?
IT BELONGS TO WERNER STAUFFACHER. HE IS AN IMPORTANT MAN HERE IN THE CANTON OF SCHWYTZ. I'M SURE HE WILL HELP YOU HIDE.
WILLIAM TELL, IS THAT YOU? WHAT ARE YOU DOING HERE SO LATE AND IN SUCH WEATHER?
THIS IS BAUMGARTEN FROM UNTERWALD. HE'S IN DEEP TROUBLE, THROUGH NO FAULT OF HIS OWN. I WAS HOPING YOU COULD GIVE HIM SHELTER.
COME IN. COME IN. I KNOW A THING OR TWO ABOUT BEING IN TROUBLE THROUGH NO FAULT OF YOUR OWN. MANY DO THESE DAYS.

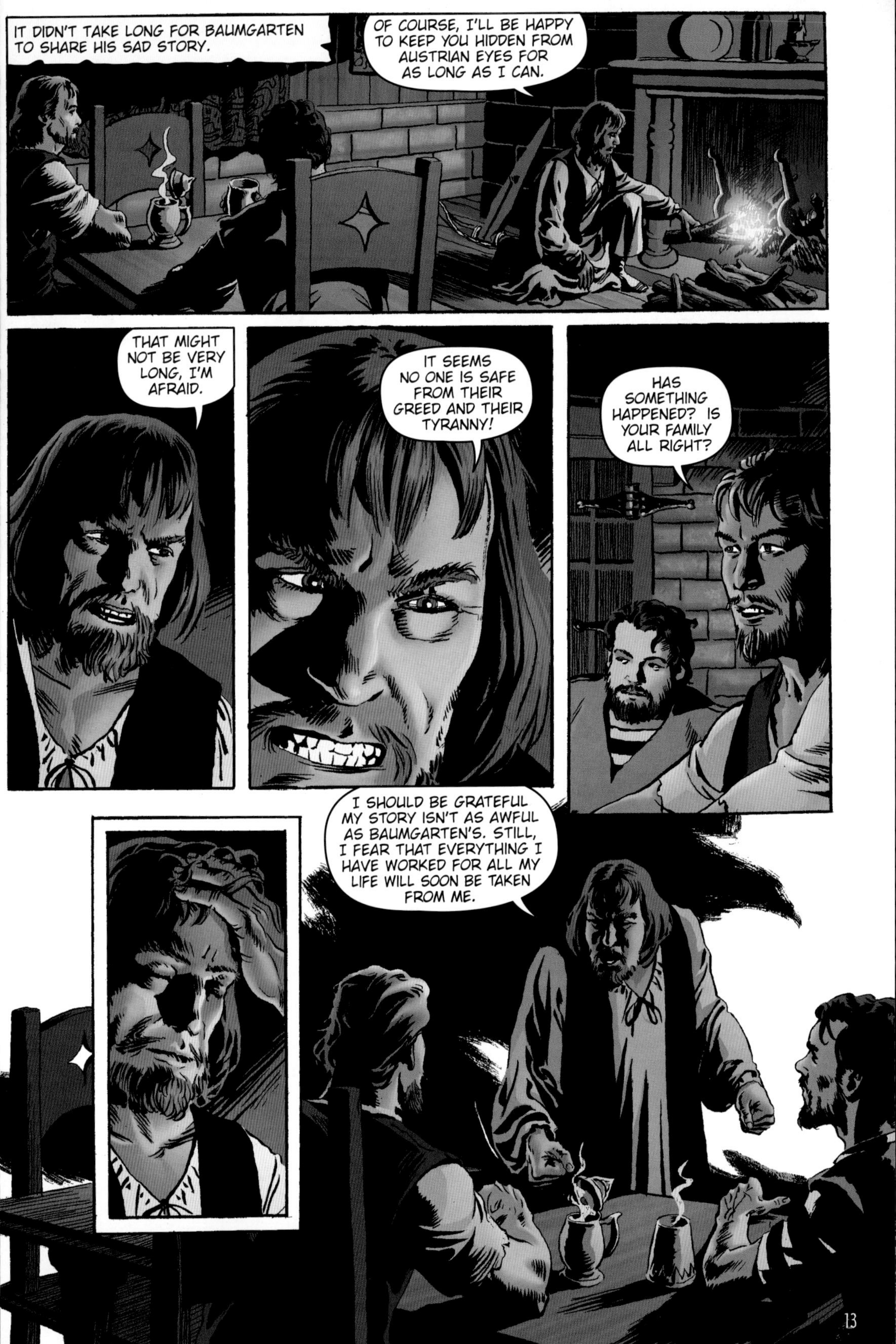
IT DIDN'T TAKE LONG FOR BAUMGARTEN TO SHARE HIS SAD STORY.
OF COURSE, I'LL BE HAPPY TO KEEP YOU HIDDEN FROM AUSTRIAN EYES FOR AS LONG AS I CAN.
THAT MIGHT NOT BE VERY LONG, I'M AFRAID.
IT SEEMS NO ONE IS SAFE FROM THEIR GREED AND THEIR TYRANNY!
HAS SOMETHING HAPPENED? IS YOUR FAMILY ALL RIGHT?
I SHOULD BE GRATEFUL MY STORY ISN'T AS AWFUL AS BAUMGARTEN'S. STILL, I FEAR THAT EVERYTHING I HAVE WORKED FOR ALL MY LIFE WILL SOON BE TAKEN FROM ME.

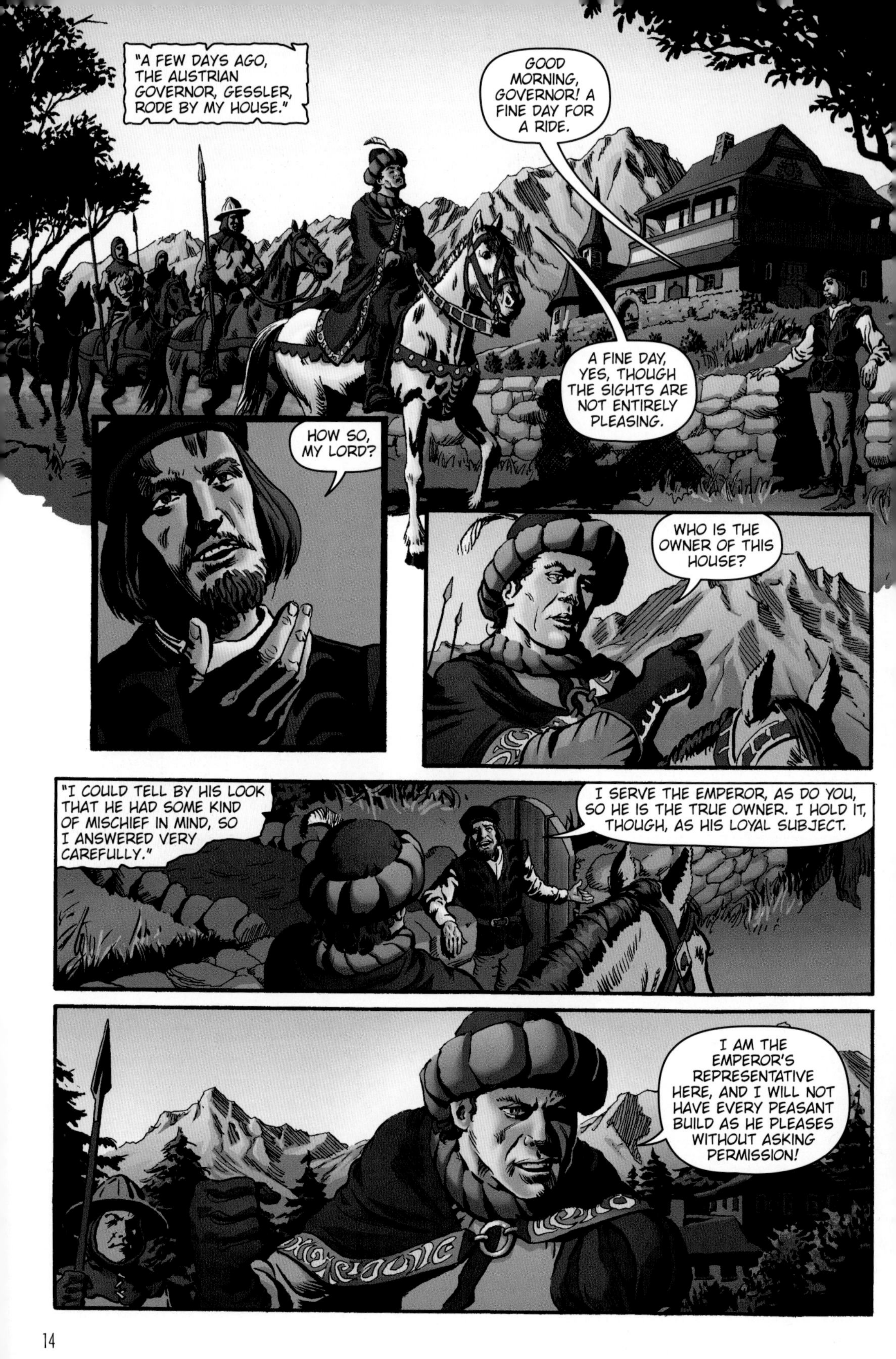
"A FEW DAYS AGO, THE AUSTRIAN GOVERNOR, GESSLER, RODE BY MY HOUSE."
GOOD MORNING, GOVERNOR! A FINE DAY FOR A RIDE.
A FINE DAY, YES, THOUGH THE SIGHTS ARE NOT ENTIRELY PLEASING.
HOW SO, MY LORD?
WHO IS THE OWNER OF THIS HOUSE?
"I COULD TELL BY HIS LOOK THAT HE HAD SOME KIND OF MISCHIEF IN MIND, SO I ANSWERED VERY CAREFULLY."
I SERVE THE EMPEROR, AS DO YOU, SO HE IS THE TRUE OWNER. I HOLD IT, THOUGH, AS HIS LOYAL SUBJECT.
I AM THE EMPEROR'S REPRESENTATIVE HERE, AND I WILL NOT HAVE EVERY PEASANT BUILD AS HE PLEASES WITHOUT ASKING PERMISSION!

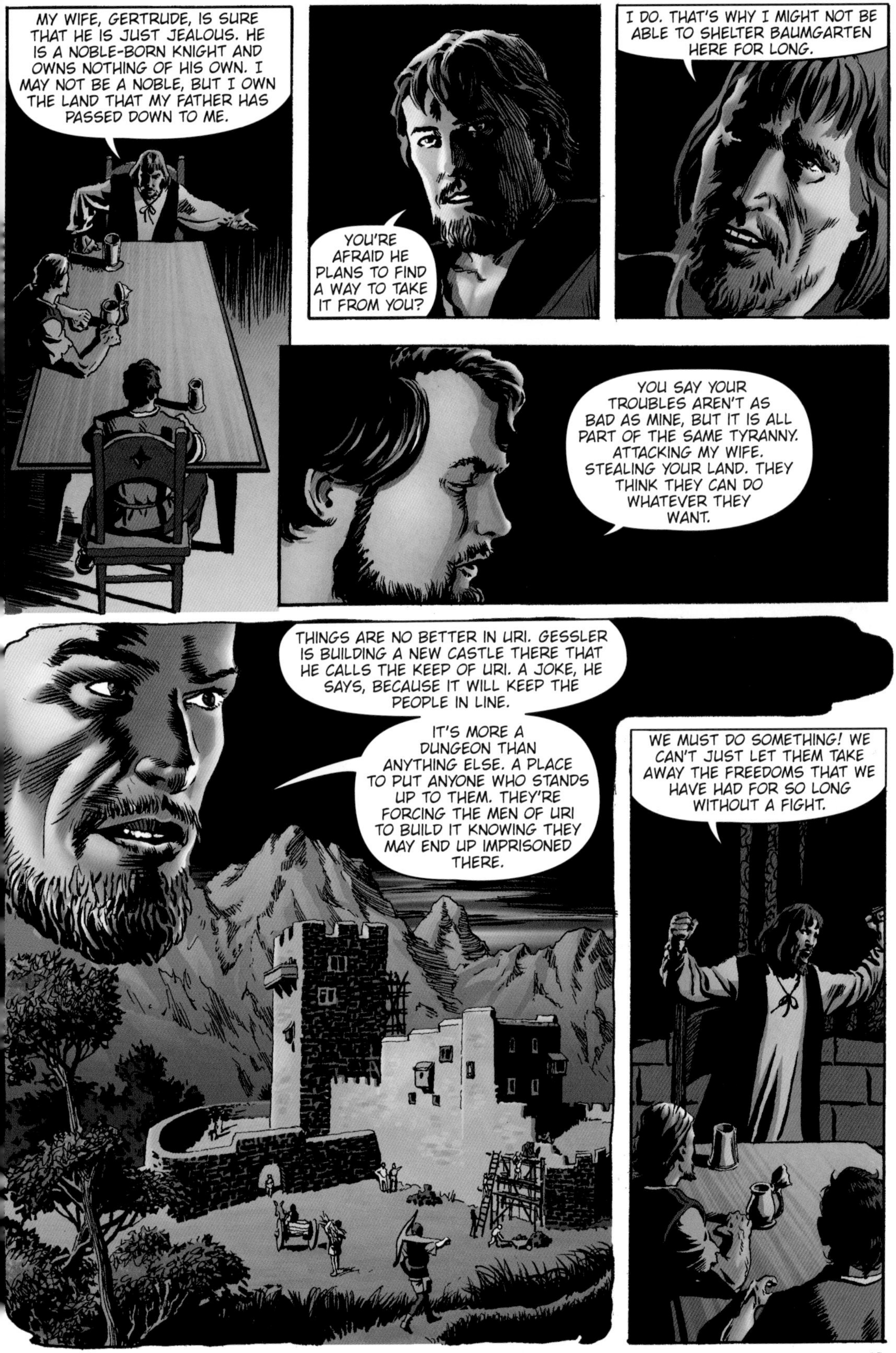
MY WIFE, GERTRUDE, IS SURE THAT HE IS JUST JEALOUS. HE IS A NOBLE-BORN KNIGHT AND OWNS NOTHING OF HIS OWN. I MAY NOT BE A NOBLE, BUT I OWN THE LAND THAT MY FATHER HAS PASSED DOWN TO ME.
YOU'RE AFRAID HE PLANS TO FIND A WAY TO TAKE IT FROM YOU?
I DO. THAT'S WHY I MIGHT NOT BE ABLE TO SHELTER BAUMGARTEN HERE FOR LONG.
YOU SAY YOUR TROUBLES AREN'T AS BAD AS MINE, BUT IT IS ALL PART OF THE SAME TYRANNY. ATTACKING MY WIFE. STEALING YOUR LAND. THEY THINK THEY CAN DO WHATEVER THEY WANT.
THINGS ARE NO BETTER IN URI. GESSLER IS BUILDING A NEW CASTLE THERE THAT HE CALLS THE KEEP OF URI. A JOKE, HE SAYS, BECAUSE IT WILL KEEP THE PEOPLE IN LINE.
IT'S MORE A DUNGEON THAN ANYTHING ELSE. A PLACE TO PUT ANYONE WHO STANDS UP TO THEM. THEY'RE FORCING THE MEN OF URI TO BUILD IT KNOWING THEY MAY END UP IMPRISONED THERE.
WE MUST DO SOMETHING! WE CAN'T JUST LET THEM TAKE AWAY THE FREEDOMS THAT WE HAVE HAD FOR SO LONG WITHOUT A FIGHT.

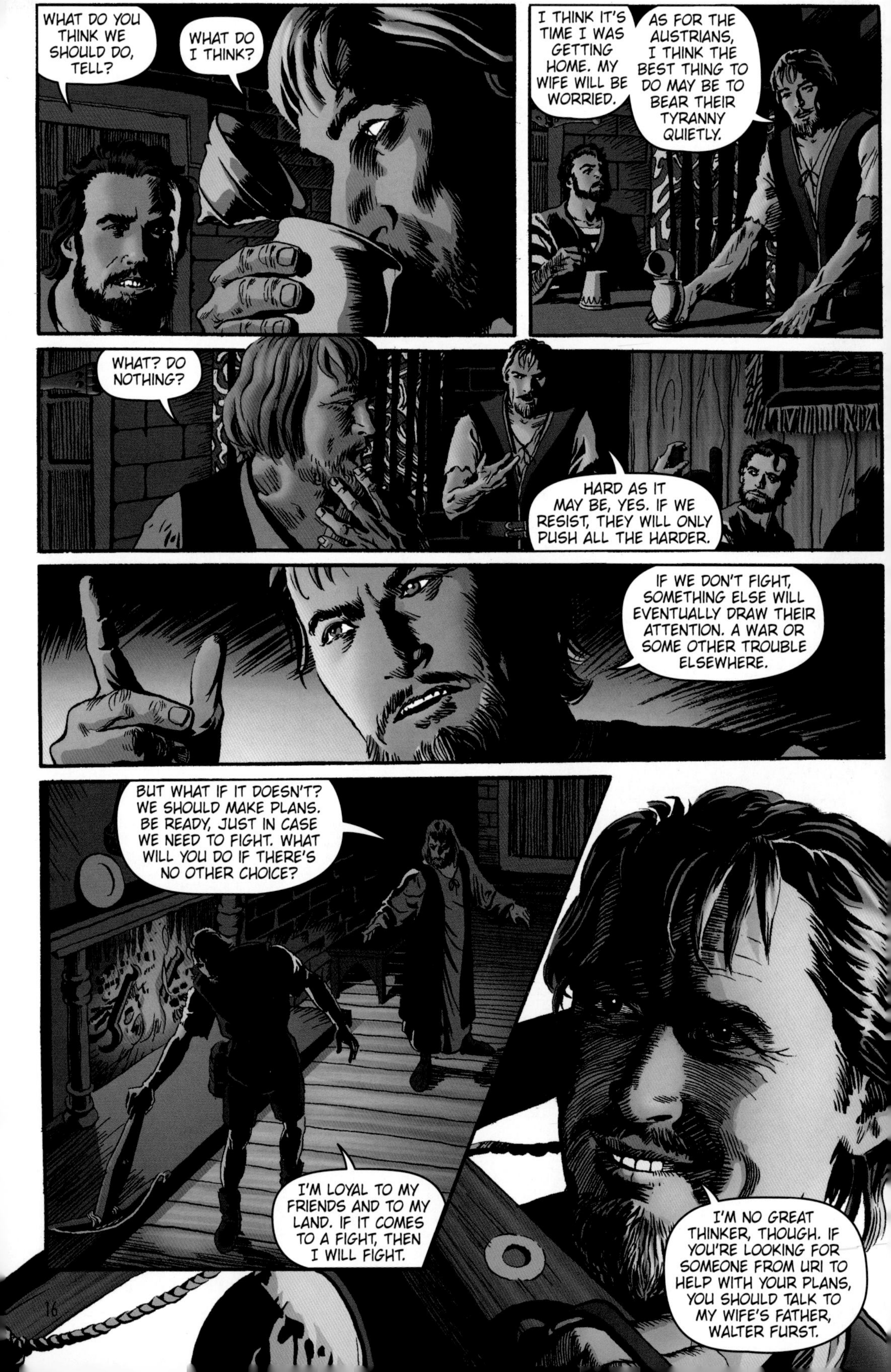
WHAT DO YOU THINK WE SHOULD DO, TELL?
WHAT DO I THINK?
I THINK IT'S TIME I WAS GETTING HOME. MY WIFE WILL BE WORRIED.
AS FOR THE AUSTRIANS, I THINK THE BEST THING TO DO MAY BE TO BEAR THEIR TYRANNY QUIETLY.
WHAT? DO NOTHING?
HARD AS IT MAY BE, YES. IF WE RESIST, THEY WILL ONLY PUSH ALL THE HARDER.
IF WE DON'T FIGHT, SOMETHING ELSE WILL EVENTUALLY DRAW THEIR ATTENTION. A WAR OR SOME OTHER TROUBLE ELSEWHERE.
BUT WHAT IF IT DOESN'T? WE SHOULD MAKE PLANS. BE READY, JUST IN CASE WE NEED TO FIGHT. WHAT WILL YOU DO IF THERE'S NO OTHER CHOICE?
I'M LOYAL TO MY FRIENDS AND TO MY LAND. IF IT COMES TO A FIGHT, THEN I WILL FIGHT.
I'M NO GREAT THINKER, THOUGH. IF YOU'RE LOOKING FOR SOMEONE FROM URI TO HELP WITH YOUR PLANS, YOU SHOULD TALK TO MY WIFE'S FATHER, WALTER FURST.

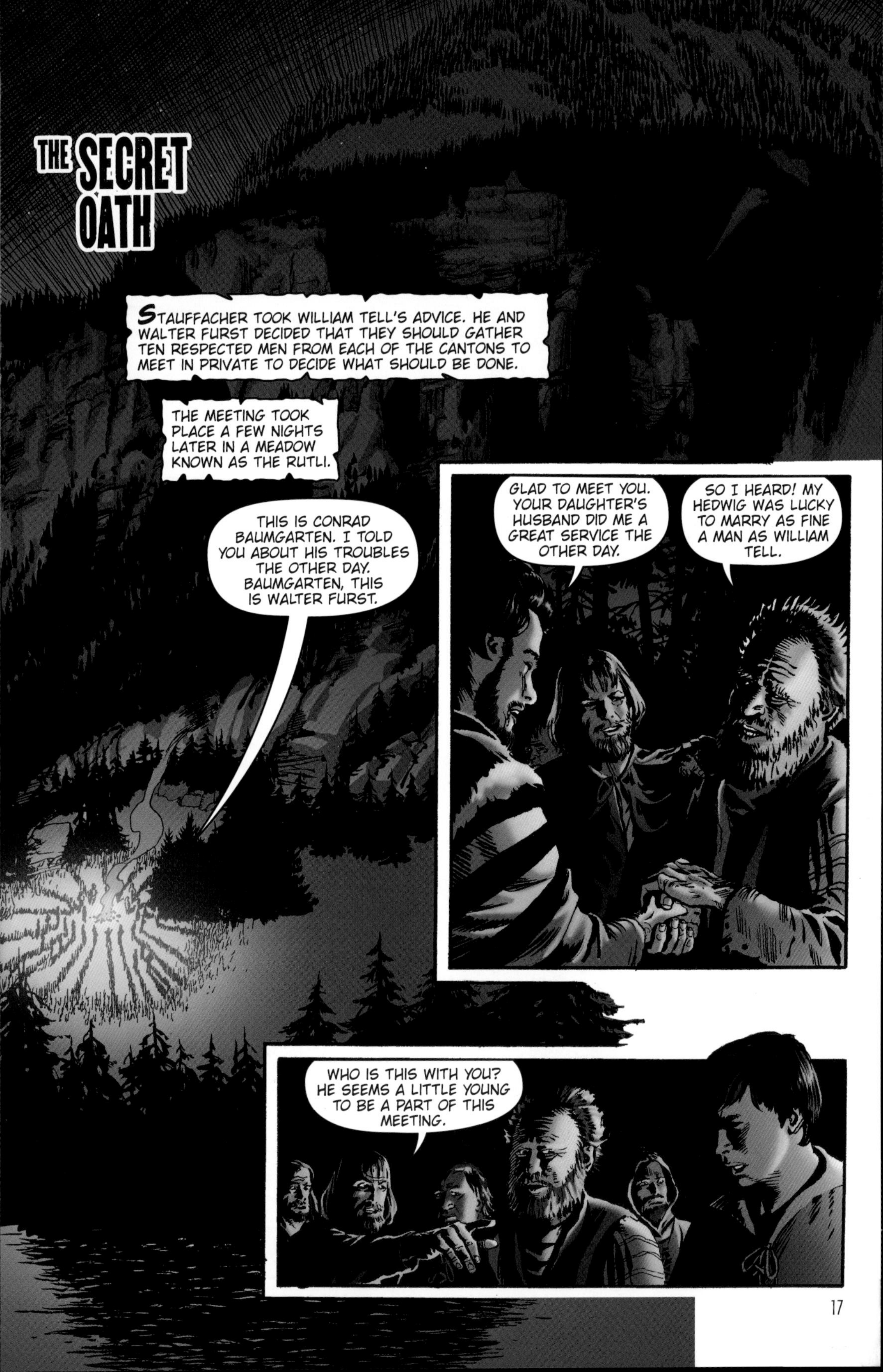
THE SECRET OATH
STAUFFACHER TOOK WILLIAM TELL'S ADVICE. HE AND WALTER FURST DECIDED THAT THEY SHOULD GATHER TEN RESPECTED MEN FROM EACH OF THE CANTONS TO MEET IN PRIVATE TO DECIDE WHAT SHOULD BE DONE.
THE MEETING TOOK PLACE A FEW NIGHTS LATER IN A MEADOW KNOWN AS THE RUTLI.
THIS IS CONRAD BAUMGARTEN. I TOLD YOU ABOUT HIS TROUBLES THE OTHER DAY. BAUMGARTEN, THIS IS WALTER FURST.
GLAD TO MEET YOU. YOUR DAUGHTER'S HUSBAND DID ME A GREAT SERVICE THE OTHER DAY.
SO I HEARD! MY HEDWIG WAS LUCKY TO MARRY AS FINE A MAN AS WILLIAM TELL.
WHO IS THIS WITH YOU? HE SEEMS A LITTLE YOUNG TO BE A PART OF THIS MEETING.

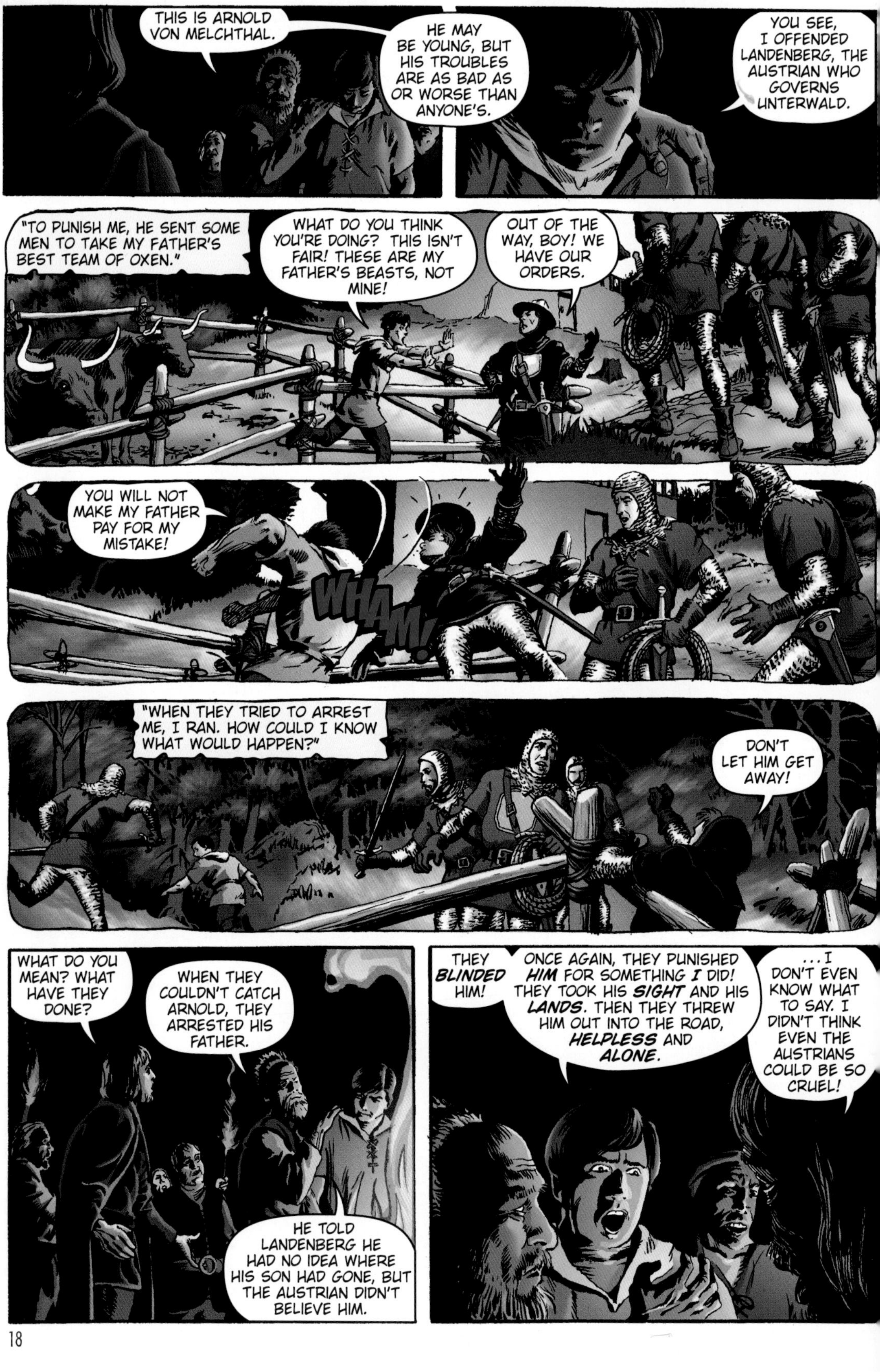
THIS IS ARNOLD VON MELCHTHAL.
HE MAY BE YOUNG, BUT HIS TROUBLES ARE AS BAD AS OR WORSE THAN ANYONE'S.
YOU SEE, I OFFENDED LANDENBERG, THE AUSTRIAN WHO GOVERNS UNTERWALD.
"TO PUNISH ME, HE SENT SOME MEN TO TAKE MY FATHER'S BEST TEAM OF OXEN."
WHAT DO YOU THINK YOU'RE DOING? THIS ISN'T FAIR! THESE ARE MY FATHER'S BEASTS, NOT MINE!
OUT OF THE WAY, BOY! WE HAVE OUR ORDERS.
YOU WILL NOT MAKE MY FATHER PAY FOR MY MISTAKE!
WHAM!
"WHEN THEY TRIED TO ARREST ME, I RAN. HOW COULD I KNOW WHAT WOULD HAPPEN?"
DON'T LET HIM GET AWAY!
WHAT DO YOU MEAN? WHAT HAVE THEY DONE?
WHEN THEY COULDN'T CATCH ARNOLD, THEY ARRESTED HIS FATHER.
HE TOLD LANDENBERG HE HAD NO IDEA WHERE HIS SON HAD GONE, BUT THE AUSTRIAN DIDN'T BELIEVE HIM.
THEY *BLINDED* HIM!
ONCE AGAIN, THEY PUNISHED ***HIM*** FOR SOMETHING ***I*** DID! THEY TOOK HIS ***SIGHT*** AND HIS ***LANDS***. THEN THEY THREW HIM OUT INTO THE ROAD, ***HELPLESS*** AND ***ALONE***.
...I DON'T EVEN KNOW WHAT TO SAY. I DIDN'T THINK EVEN THE AUSTRIANS COULD BE SO CRUEL!

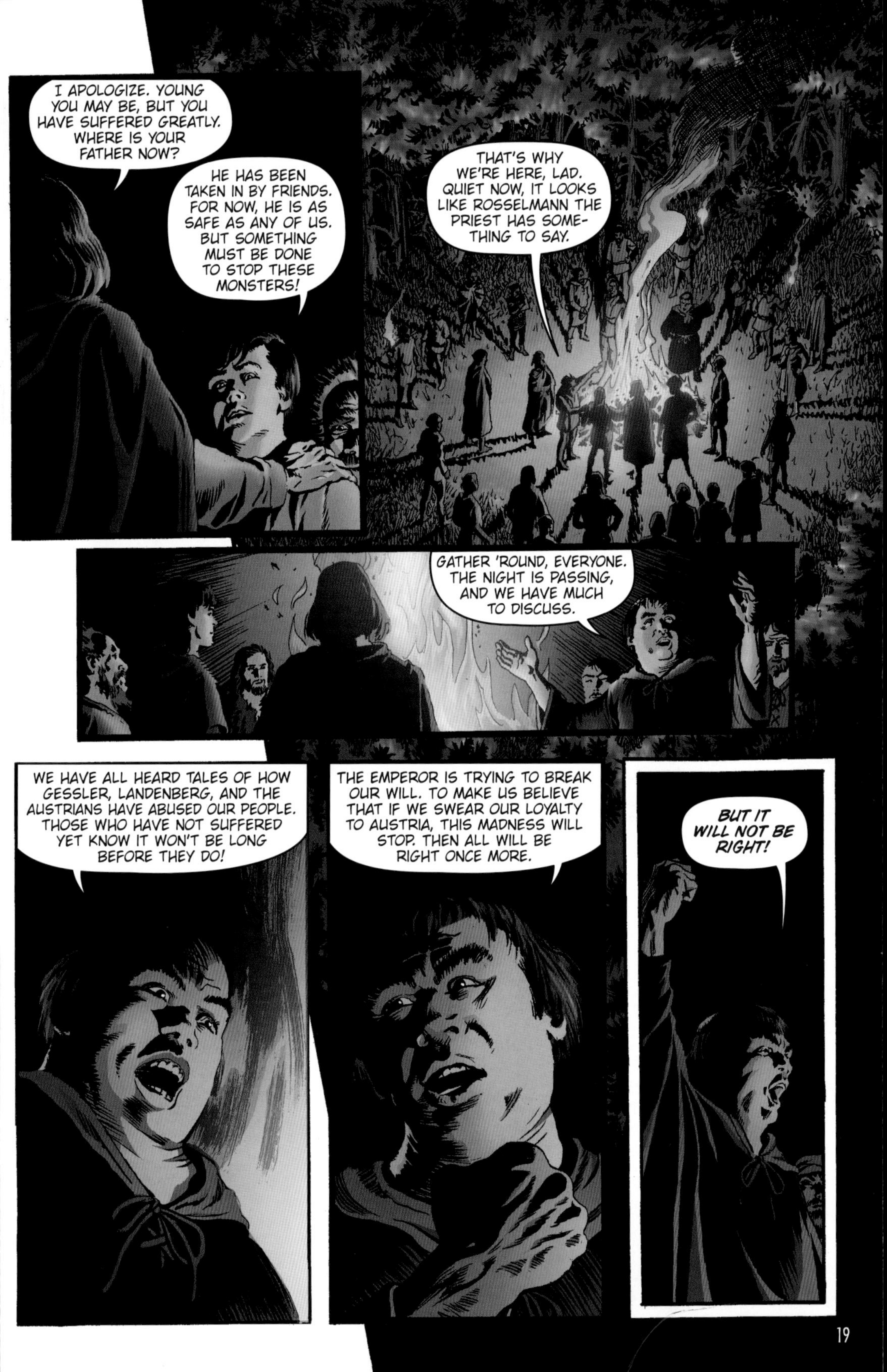

I APOLOGIZE. YOUNG YOU MAY BE, BUT YOU HAVE SUFFERED GREATLY. WHERE IS YOUR FATHER NOW?
HE HAS BEEN TAKEN IN BY FRIENDS. FOR NOW, HE IS AS SAFE AS ANY OF US. BUT SOMETHING MUST BE DONE TO STOP THESE MONSTERS!
THAT'S WHY WE'RE HERE, LAD. QUIET NOW, IT LOOKS LIKE ROSSELMANN THE PRIEST HAS SOME-THING TO SAY.
GATHER 'ROUND, EVERYONE. THE NIGHT IS PASSING, AND WE HAVE MUCH TO DISCUSS.
WE HAVE ALL HEARD TALES OF HOW GESSLER, LANDENBERG, AND THE AUSTRIANS HAVE ABUSED OUR PEOPLE. THOSE WHO HAVE NOT SUFFERED YET KNOW IT WON'T BE LONG BEFORE THEY DO!
THE EMPEROR IS TRYING TO BREAK OUR WILL. TO MAKE US BELIEVE THAT IF WE SWEAR OUR LOYALTY TO AUSTRIA, THIS MADNESS WILL STOP. THEN ALL WILL BE RIGHT ONCE MORE.
BUT IT WILL NOT BE RIGHT!

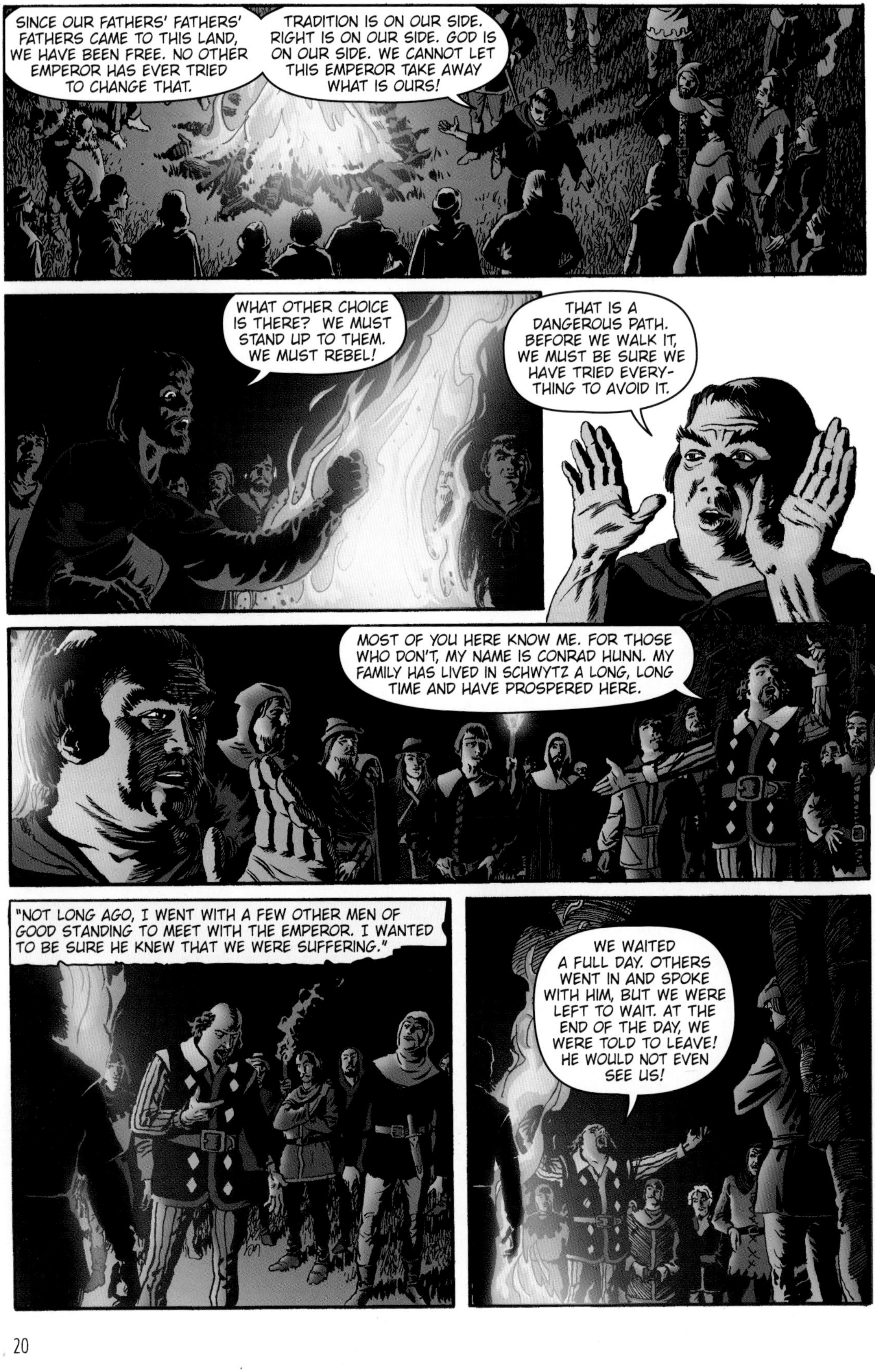
SINCE OUR FATHERS' FATHERS' FATHERS CAME TO THIS LAND, WE HAVE BEEN FREE. NO OTHER EMPEROR HAS EVER TRIED TO CHANGE THAT.
TRADITION IS ON OUR SIDE. RIGHT IS ON OUR SIDE. GOD IS ON OUR SIDE. WE CANNOT LET THIS EMPEROR TAKE AWAY WHAT IS OURS!
WHAT OTHER CHOICE IS THERE? WE MUST STAND UP TO THEM. WE MUST REBEL!
THAT IS A DANGEROUS PATH. BEFORE WE WALK IT, WE MUST BE SURE WE HAVE TRIED EVERYTHING TO AVOID IT.
MOST OF YOU HERE KNOW ME. FOR THOSE WHO DON'T, MY NAME IS CONRAD HUNN. MY FAMILY HAS LIVED IN SCHWYTZ A LONG, LONG TIME AND HAVE PROSPERED HERE.
"NOT LONG AGO, I WENT WITH A FEW OTHER MEN OF GOOD STANDING TO MEET WITH THE EMPEROR. I WANTED TO BE SURE HE KNEW THAT WE WERE SUFFERING."
WE WAITED A FULL DAY. OTHERS WENT IN AND SPOKE WITH HIM, BUT WE WERE LEFT TO WAIT. AT THE END OF THE DAY, WE WERE TOLD TO LEAVE! HE WOULD NOT EVEN SEE US!

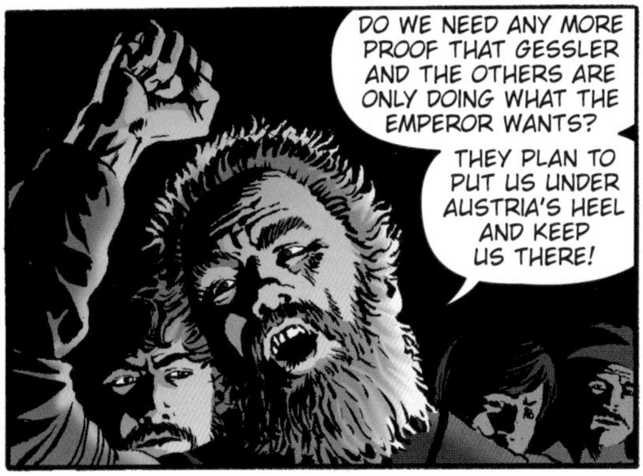
DO WE NEED ANY MORE PROOF THAT GESSLER AND THE OTHERS ARE ONLY DOING WHAT THE EMPEROR WANTS?
THEY PLAN TO PUT US UNDER AUSTRIA'S HEEL AND KEEP US THERE!

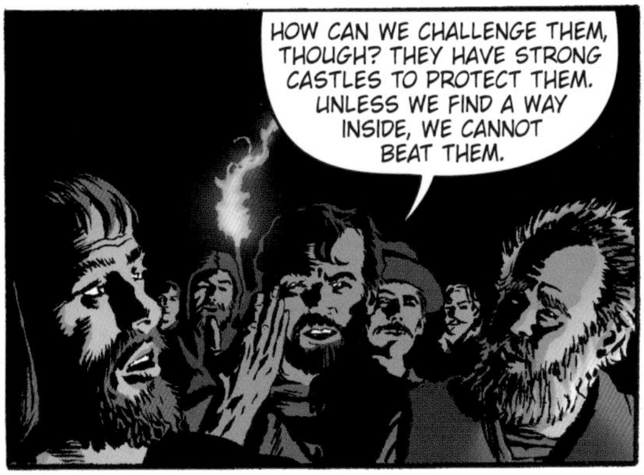
HOW CAN WE CHALLENGE THEM, THOUGH? THEY HAVE STRONG CASTLES TO PROTECT THEM. UNLESS WE FIND A WAY INSIDE, WE CANNOT BEAT THEM.

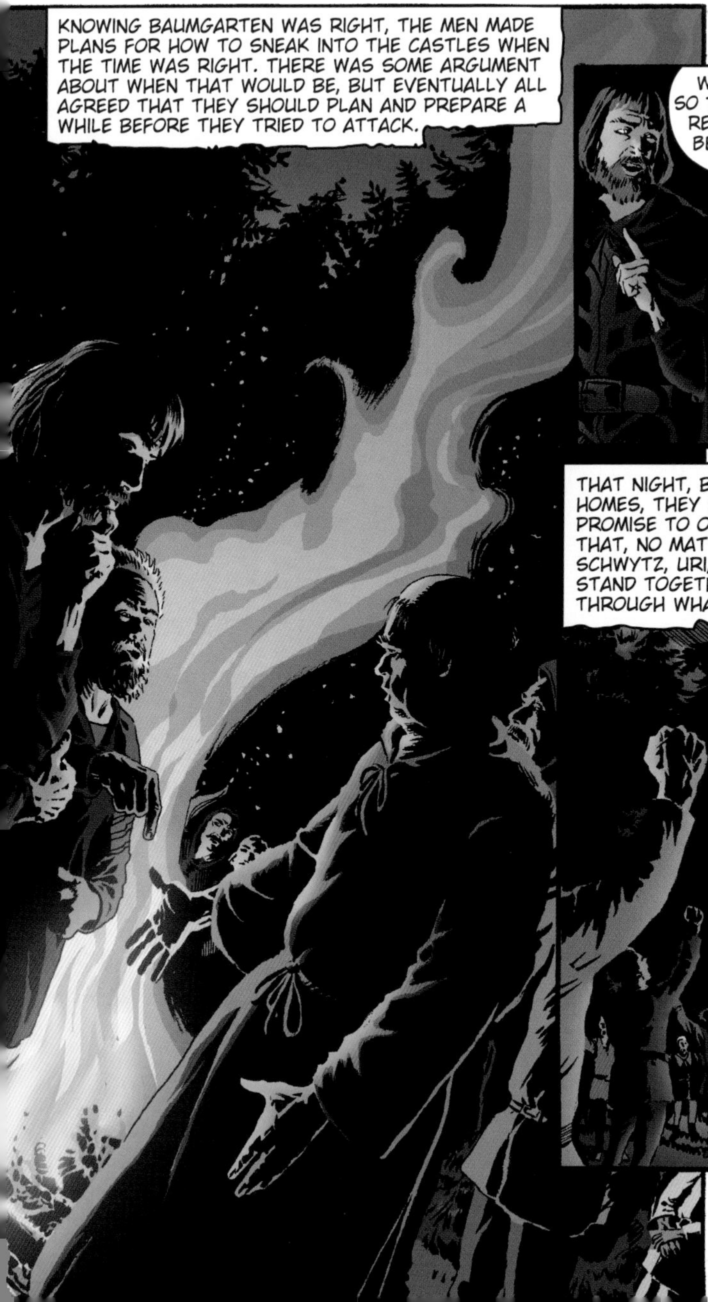
KNOWING BAUMGARTEN WAS RIGHT, THE MEN MADE PLANS FOR HOW TO SNEAK INTO THE CASTLES WHEN THE TIME WAS RIGHT. THERE WAS SOME ARGUMENT ABOUT WHEN THAT WOULD BE, BUT EVENTUALLY ALL AGREED THAT THEY SHOULD PLAN AND PREPARE A WHILE BEFORE THEY TRIED TO ATTACK.

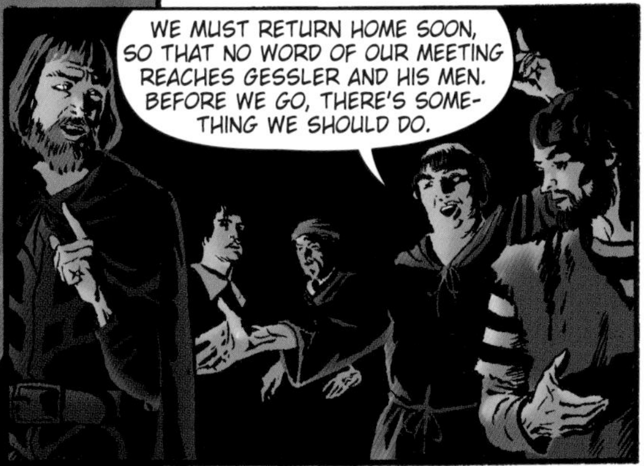
WE MUST RETURN HOME SOON, SO THAT NO WORD OF OUR MEETING REACHES GESSLER AND HIS MEN. BEFORE WE GO, THERE'S SOME-THING WE SHOULD DO.

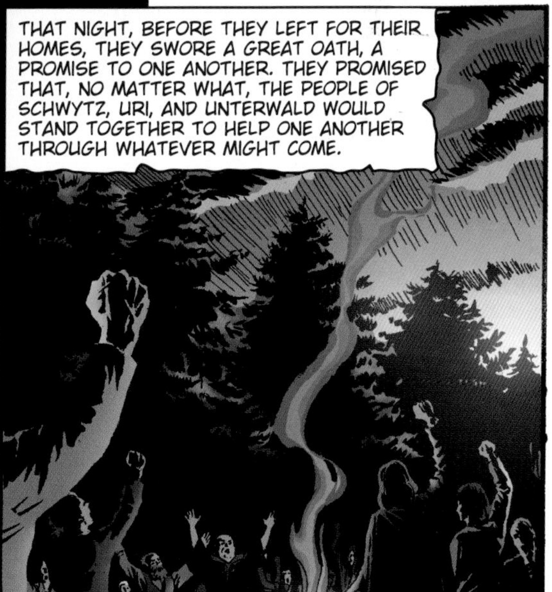
THAT NIGHT, BEFORE THEY LEFT FOR THEIR HOMES, THEY SWORE A GREAT OATH, A PROMISE TO ONE ANOTHER. THEY PROMISED THAT, NO MATTER WHAT, THE PEOPLE OF SCHWYTZ, URI, AND UNTERWALD WOULD STAND TOGETHER TO HELP ONE ANOTHER THROUGH WHATEVER MIGHT COME.

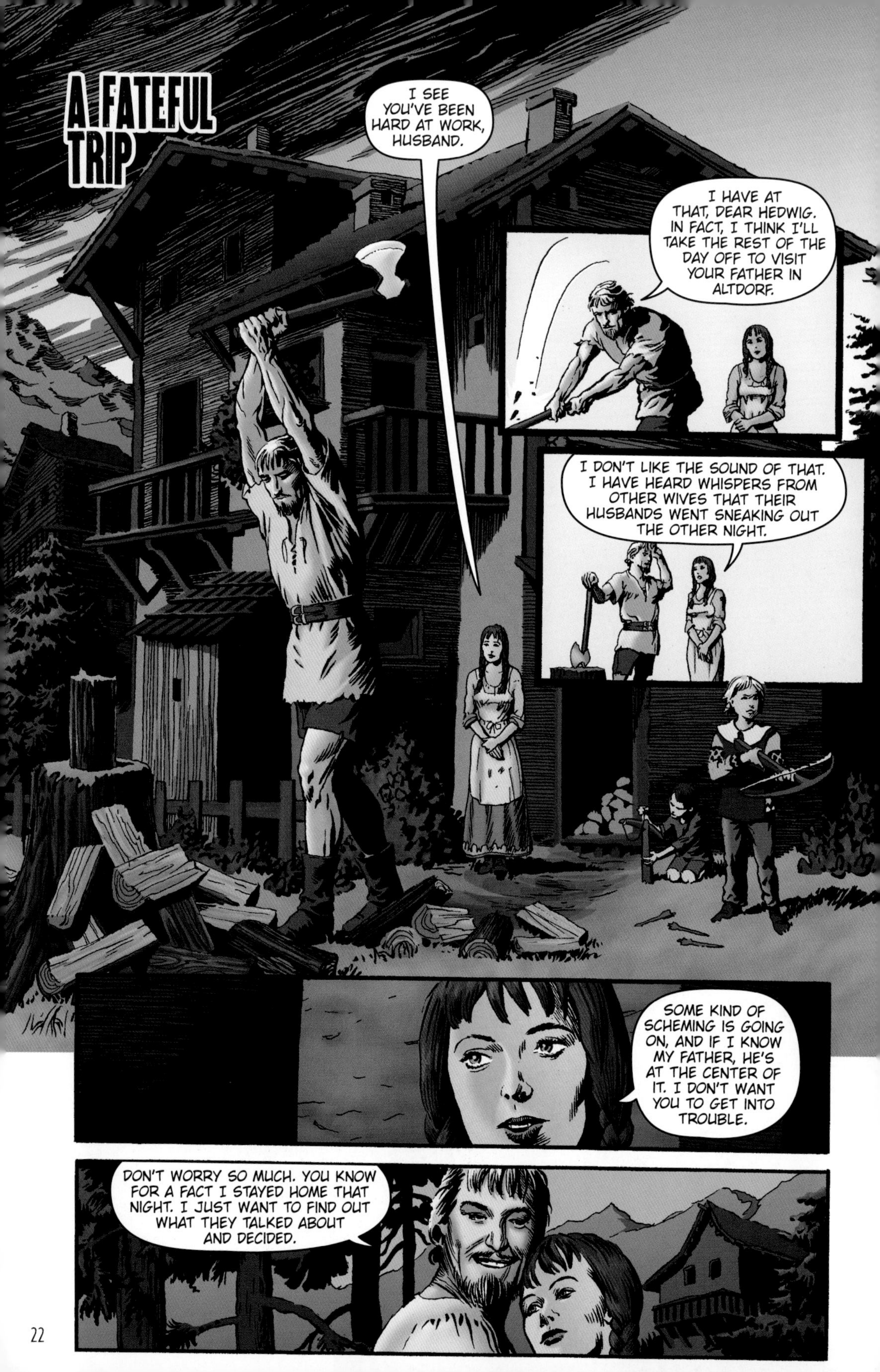
A FATEFUL TRIP
I SEE YOU'VE BEEN HARD AT WORK, HUSBAND.
I HAVE AT THAT, DEAR HEDWIG. IN FACT, I THINK I'LL TAKE THE REST OF THE DAY OFF TO VISIT YOUR FATHER IN ALTDORF.
I DON'T LIKE THE SOUND OF THAT. I HAVE HEARD WHISPERS FROM OTHER WIVES THAT THEIR HUSBANDS WENT SNEAKING OUT THE OTHER NIGHT.
SOME KIND OF SCHEMING IS GOING ON, AND IF I KNOW MY FATHER, HE'S AT THE CENTER OF IT. I DON'T WANT YOU TO GET INTO TROUBLE.
DON'T WORRY SO MUCH. YOU KNOW FOR A FACT I STAYED HOME THAT NIGHT. I JUST WANT TO FIND OUT WHAT THEY TALKED ABOUT AND DECIDED.

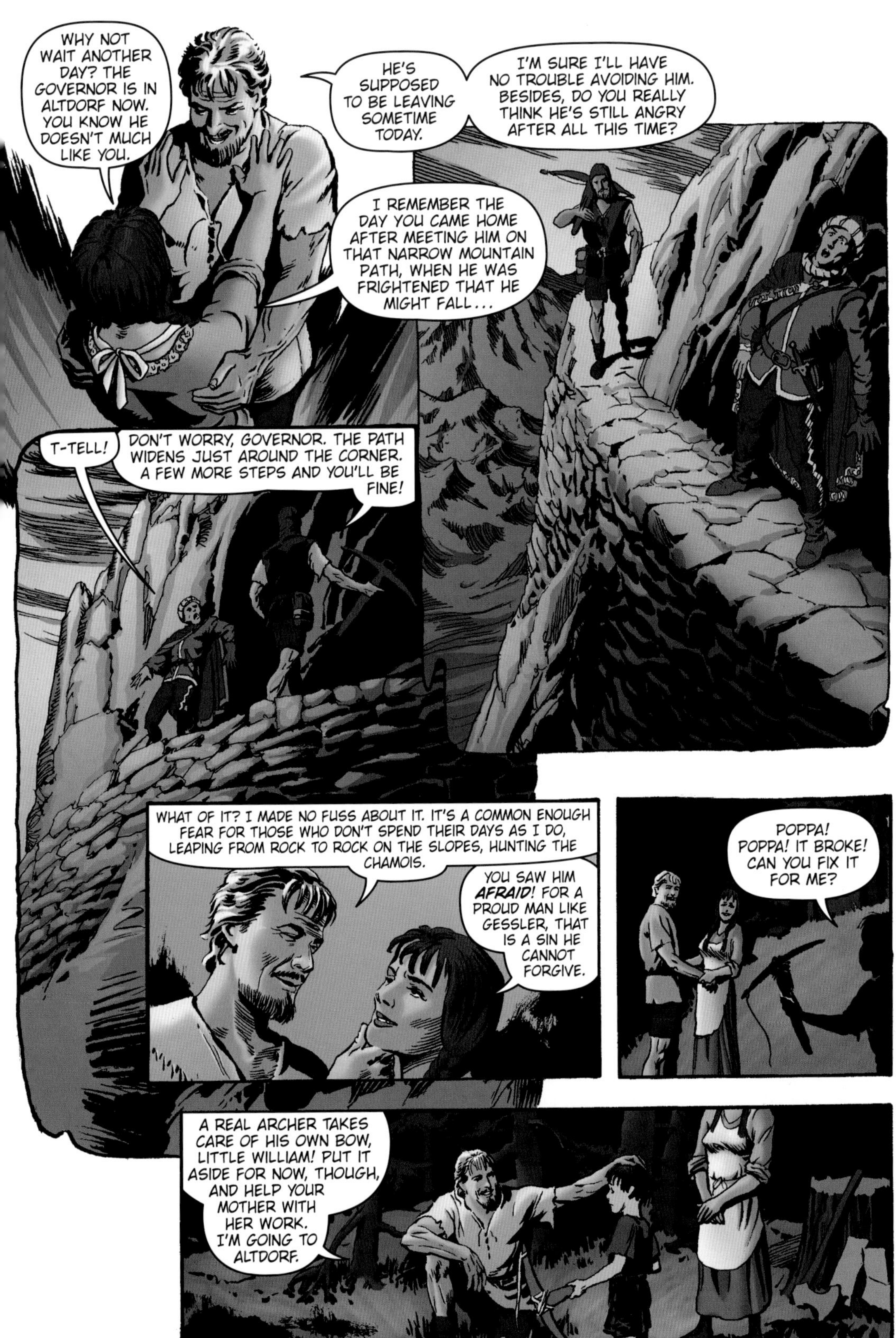

WHY NOT WAIT ANOTHER DAY? THE GOVERNOR IS IN ALTDORF NOW. YOU KNOW HE DOESN'T MUCH LIKE YOU.
HE'S SUPPOSED TO BE LEAVING SOMETIME TODAY.
I'M SURE I'LL HAVE NO TROUBLE AVOIDING HIM. BESIDES, DO YOU REALLY THINK HE'S STILL ANGRY AFTER ALL THIS TIME?
I REMEMBER THE DAY YOU CAME HOME AFTER MEETING HIM ON THAT NARROW MOUNTAIN PATH, WHEN HE WAS FRIGHTENED THAT HE MIGHT FALL...
T-TELL!
DON'T WORRY, GOVERNOR. THE PATH WIDENS JUST AROUND THE CORNER. A FEW MORE STEPS AND YOU'LL BE FINE!
WHAT OF IT? I MADE NO FUSS ABOUT IT. IT'S A COMMON ENOUGH FEAR FOR THOSE WHO DON'T SPEND THEIR DAYS AS I DO, LEAPING FROM ROCK TO ROCK ON THE SLOPES, HUNTING THE CHAMOIS.
YOU SAW HIM AFRAID! FOR A PROUD MAN LIKE GESSLER, THAT IS A SIN HE CANNOT FORGIVE.
POPPA! POPPA! IT BROKE! CAN YOU FIX IT FOR ME?
A REAL ARCHER TAKES CARE OF HIS OWN BOW, LITTLE WILLIAM! PUT IT ASIDE FOR NOW, THOUGH, AND HELP YOUR MOTHER WITH HER WORK. I'M GOING TO ALTDORF.

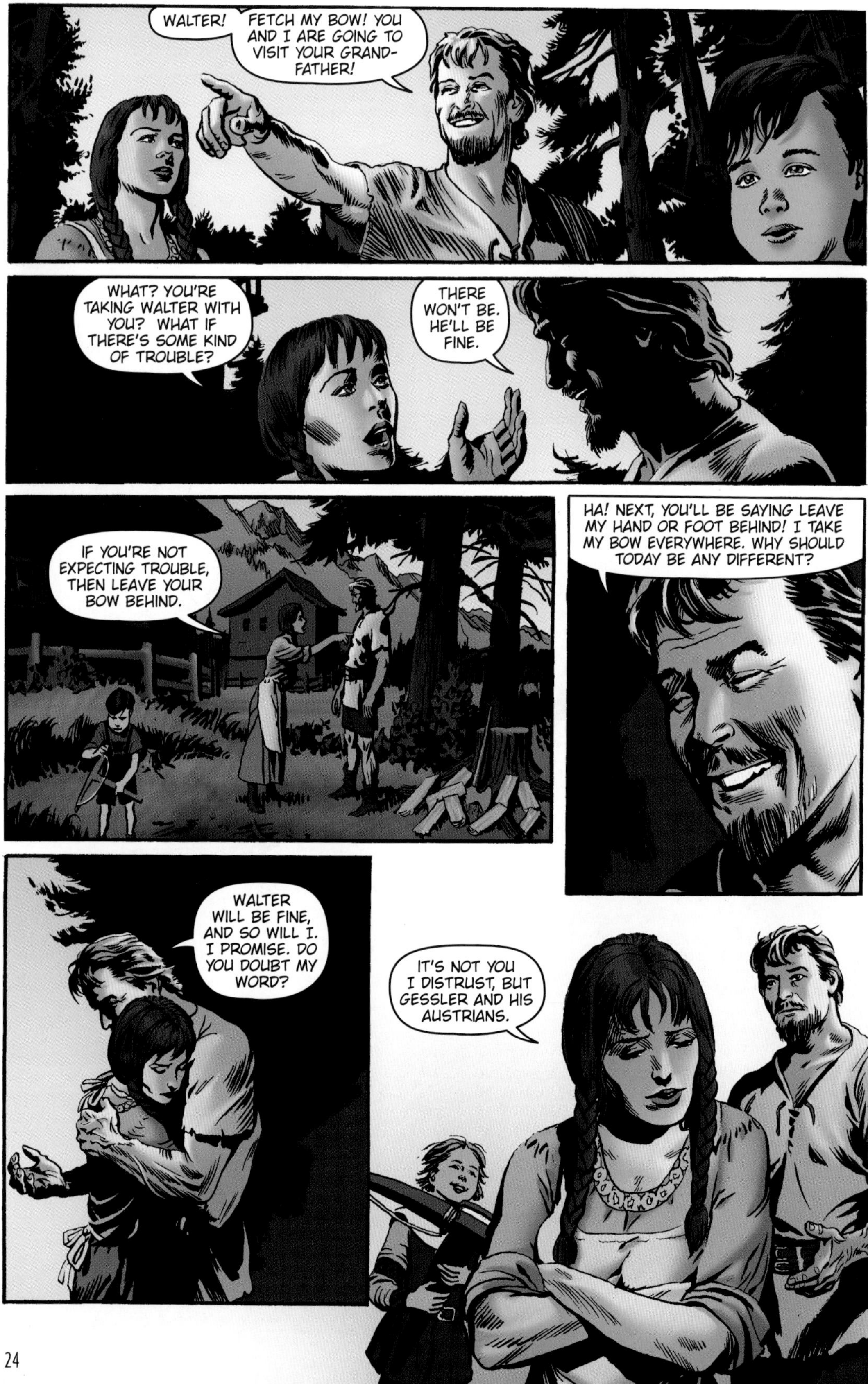
WALTER!
FETCH MY BOW! YOU AND I ARE GOING TO VISIT YOUR GRAND-FATHER!
WHAT? YOU'RE TAKING WALTER WITH YOU? WHAT IF THERE'S SOME KIND OF TROUBLE?
THERE WON'T BE. HE'LL BE FINE.
IF YOU'RE NOT EXPECTING TROUBLE, THEN LEAVE YOUR BOW BEHIND.
HA! NEXT, YOU'LL BE SAYING LEAVE MY HAND OR FOOT BEHIND! I TAKE MY BOW EVERYWHERE. WHY SHOULD TODAY BE ANY DIFFERENT?
WALTER WILL BE FINE, AND SO WILL I. I PROMISE. DO YOU DOUBT MY WORD?
IT'S NOT YOU I DISTRUST, BUT GESSLER AND HIS AUSTRIANS.

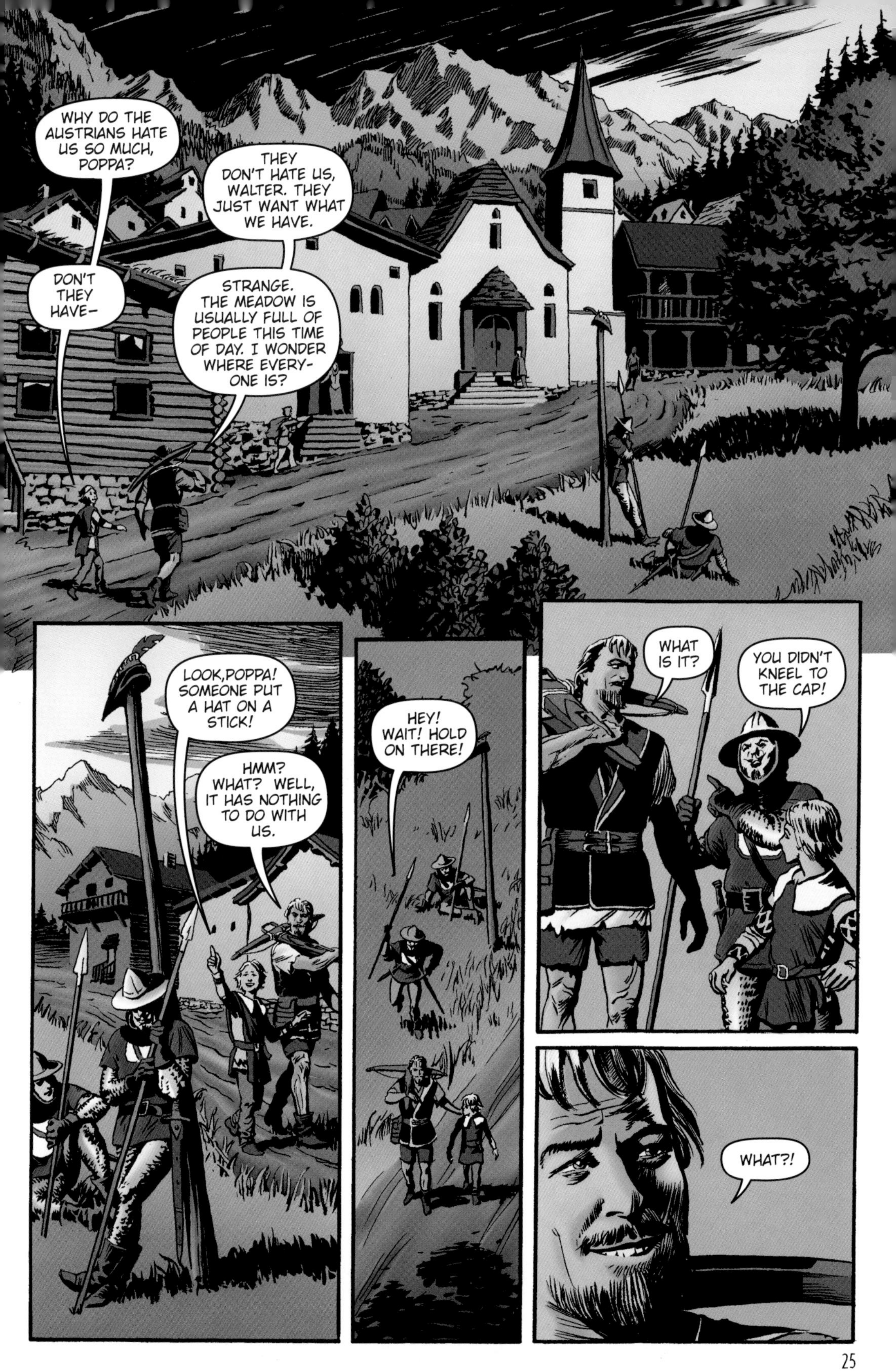
WHY DO THE AUSTRIANS HATE US SO MUCH, POPPA?
THEY DON'T HATE US, WALTER. THEY JUST WANT WHAT WE HAVE.
DON'T THEY HAVE-
STRANGE. THE MEADOW IS USUALLY FULL OF PEOPLE THIS TIME OF DAY. I WONDER WHERE EVERY-ONE IS?
LOOK,POPPA! SOMEONE PUT A HAT ON A STICK!
HMM? WHAT? WELL, IT HAS NOTHING TO DO WITH US.
HEY! WAIT! HOLD ON THERE!
WHAT IS IT?
YOU DIDN'T KNEEL TO THE CAP!
WHAT?!

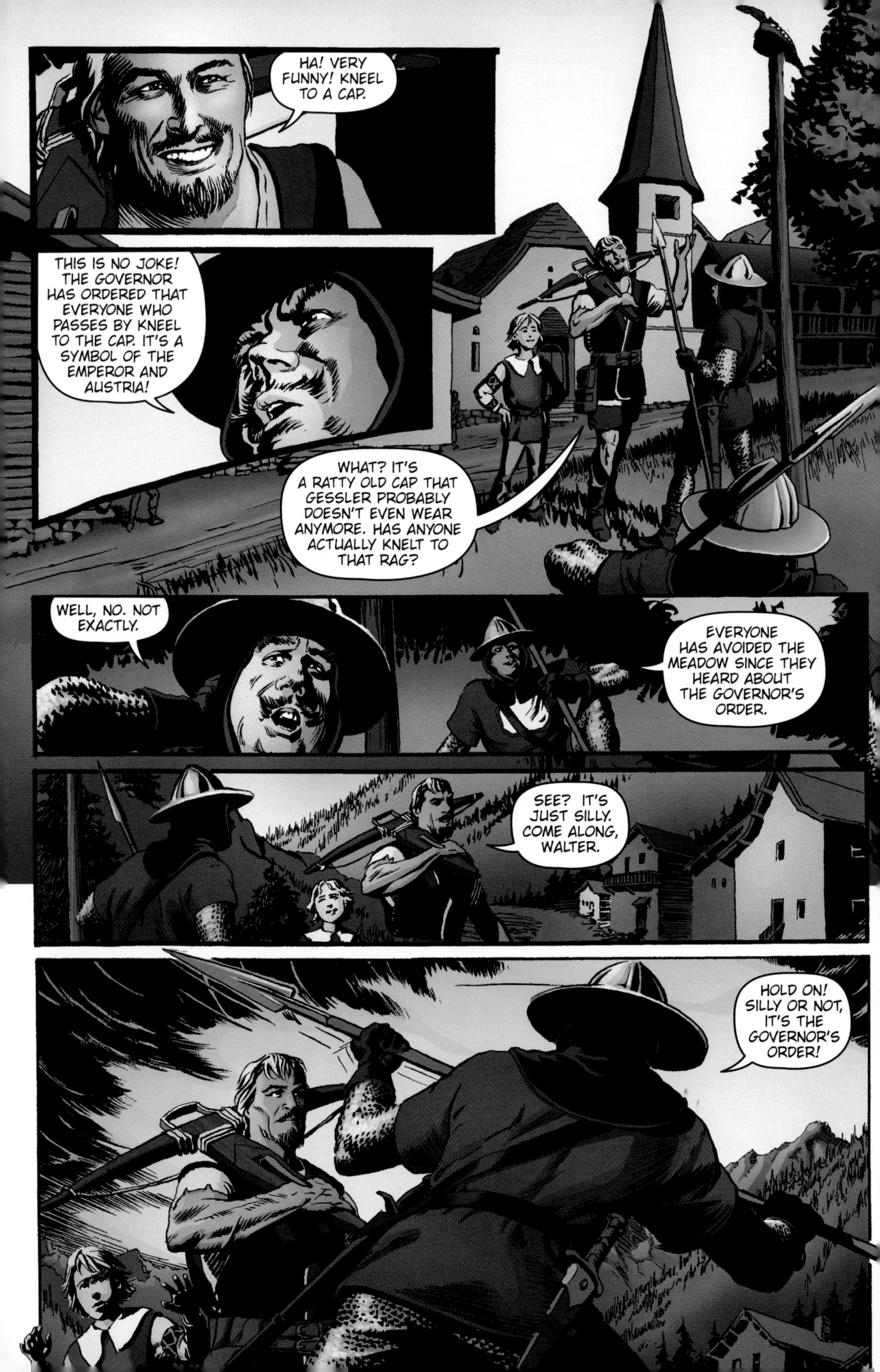
HA! VERY FUNNY! KNEEL TO A CAP.
THIS IS NO JOKE! THE GOVERNOR HAS ORDERED THAT EVERYONE WHO PASSES BY KNEEL TO THE CAP. IT'S A SYMBOL OF THE EMPEROR AND AUSTRIA!
WHAT? IT'S A RATTY OLD CAP THAT GESSLER PROBABLY DOESN'T EVEN WEAR ANYMORE. HAS ANYONE ACTUALLY KNELT TO THAT RAG?
WELL, NO. NOT EXACTLY.
EVERYONE HAS AVOIDED THE MEADOW SINCE THEY HEARD ABOUT THE GOVERNOR'S ORDER.
SEE? IT'S JUST SILLY. COME ALONG, WALTER.
HOLD ON! SILLY OR NOT, IT'S THE GOVERNOR'S ORDER!

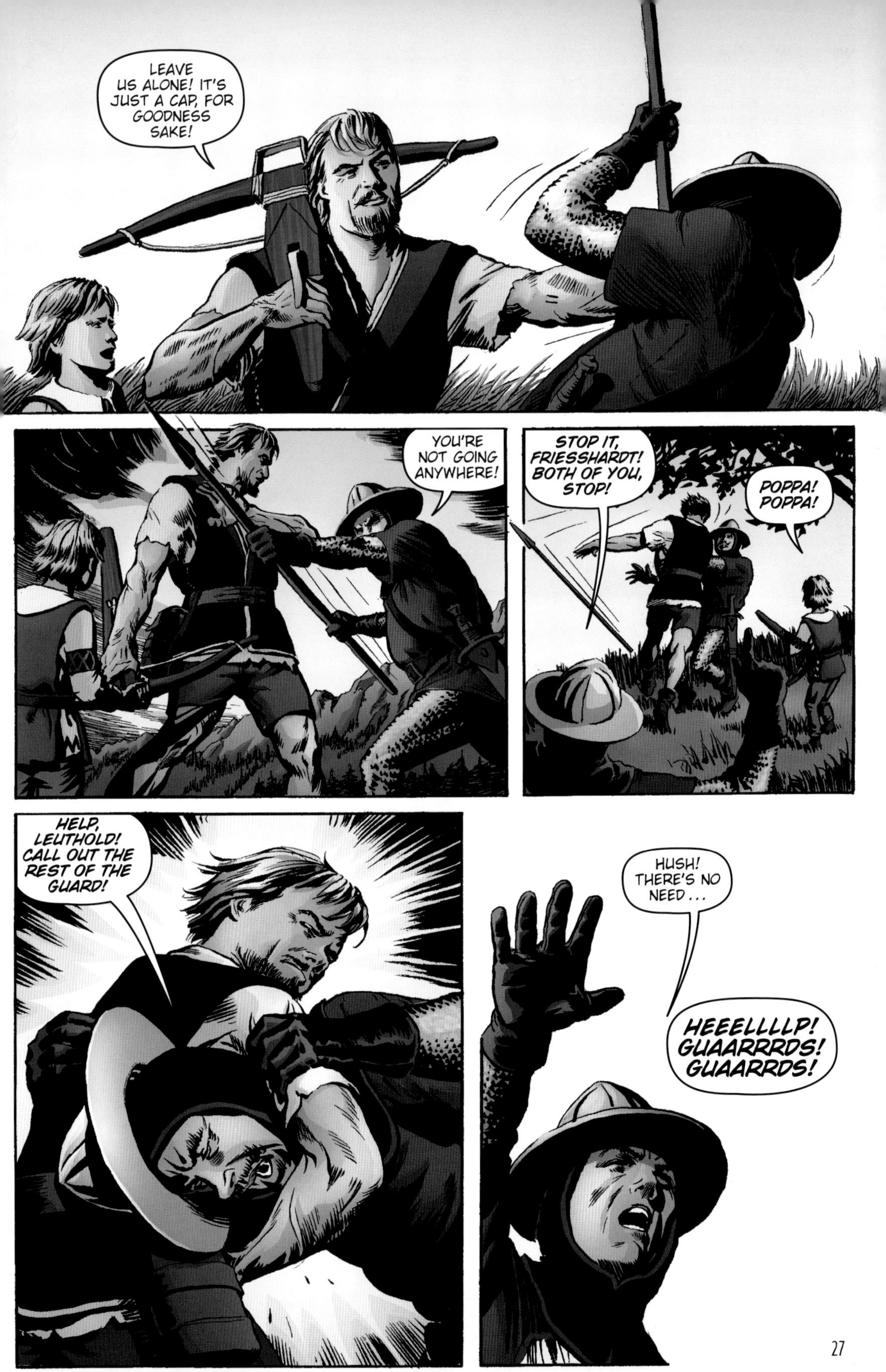

LEAVE US ALONE! IT'S JUST A CAP, FOR GOODNESS SAKE!
YOU'RE NOT GOING ANYWHERE!
STOP IT, FRIESSHARDT! BOTH OF YOU, STOP!
POPPA! POPPA!
HELP, LEUTHOLD! CALL OUT THE REST OF THE GUARD!
HUSH! THERE'S NO NEED . . .
HEEELLLLP! GUAARRRDS! GUAARRDS!

AN IMPOSSIBLE SHOT

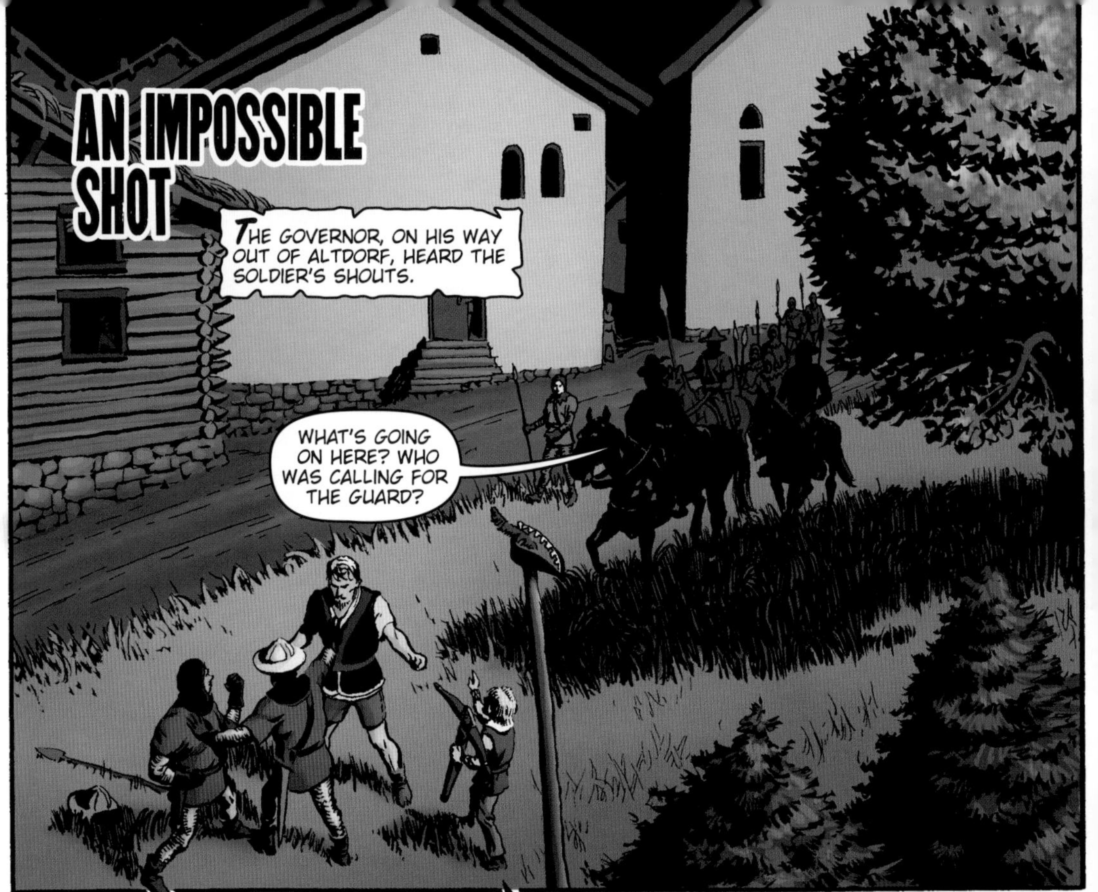
THE GOVERNOR, ON HIS WAY OUT OF ALTDORF, HEARD THE SOLDIER'S SHOUTS.
WHAT'S GOING ON HERE? WHO WAS CALLING FOR THE GUARD?

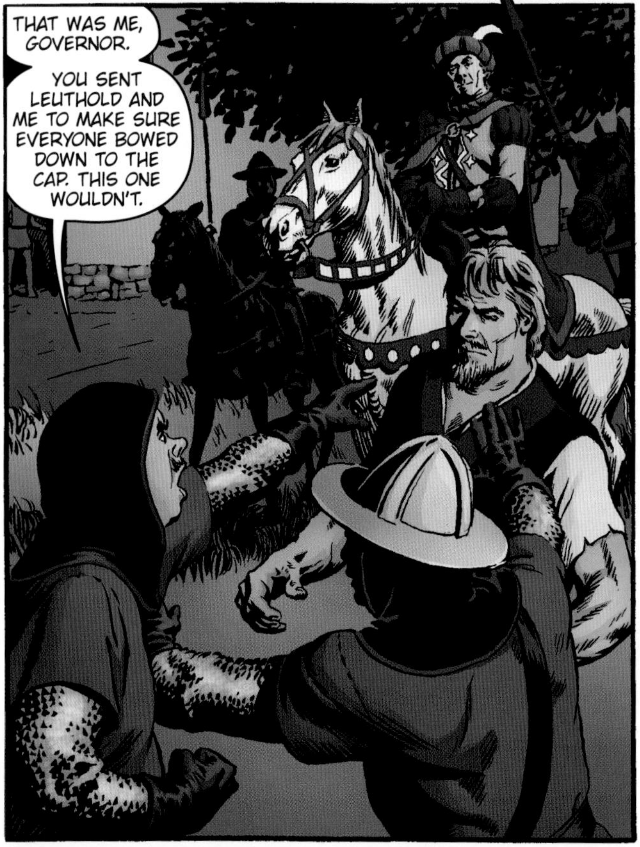
THAT WAS ME, GOVERNOR.
YOU SENT LEUTHOLD AND ME TO MAKE SURE EVERYONE BOWED DOWN TO THE CAP. THIS ONE WOULDN'T.

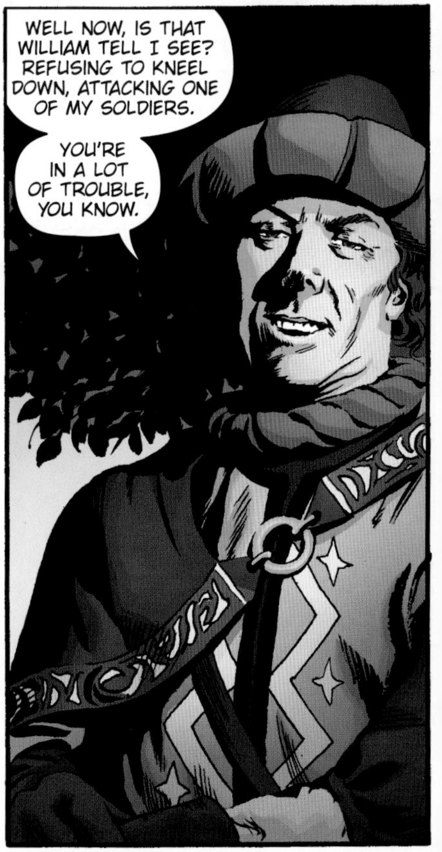
WELL NOW, IS THAT WILLIAM TELL I SEE? REFUSING TO KNEEL DOWN, ATTACKING ONE OF MY SOLDIERS.
YOU'RE IN A LOT OF TROUBLE, YOU KNOW.

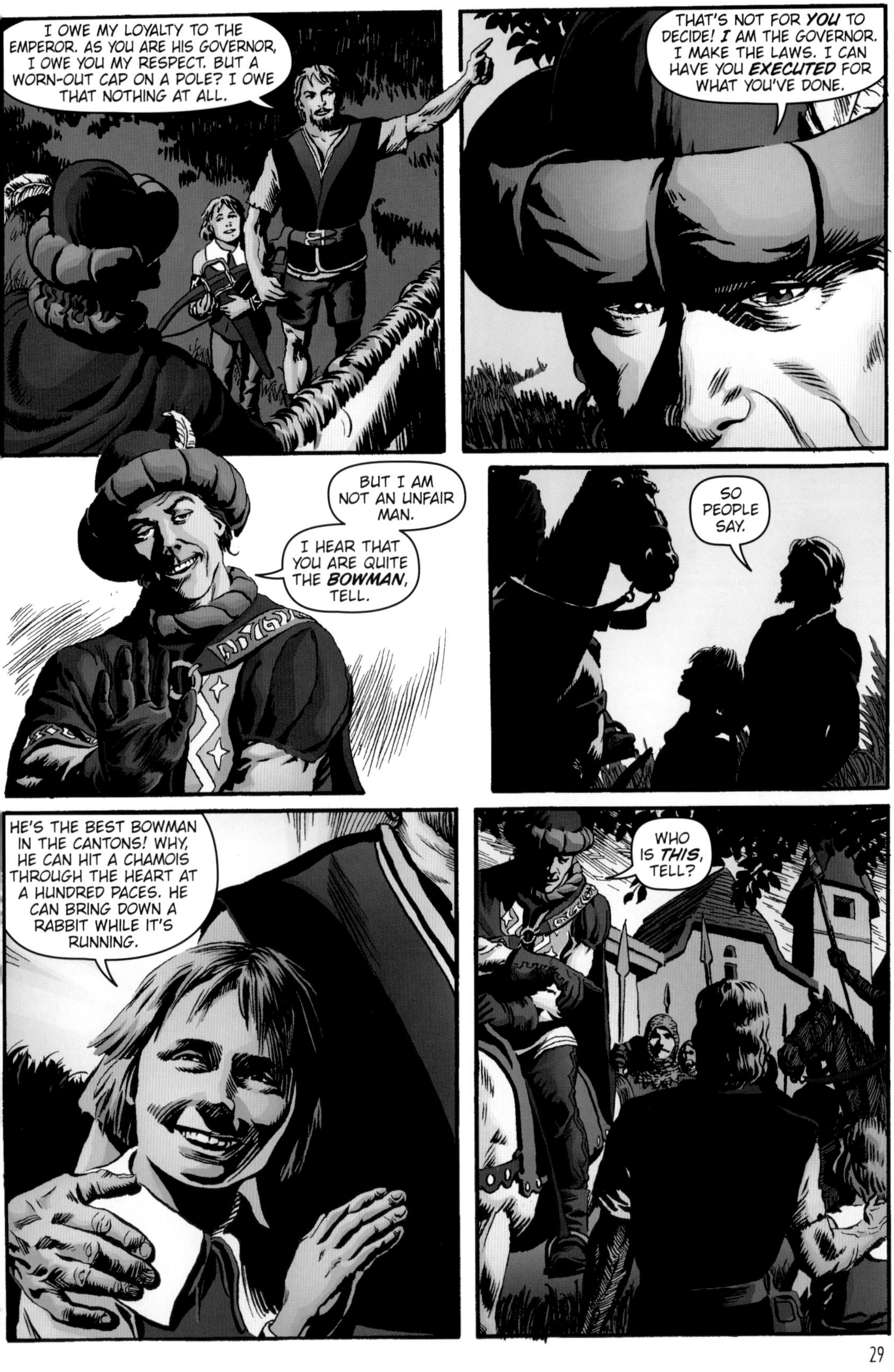
I OWE MY LOYALTY TO THE EMPEROR. AS YOU ARE HIS GOVERNOR, I OWE YOU MY RESPECT. BUT A WORN-OUT CAP ON A POLE? I OWE THAT NOTHING AT ALL.
THAT'S NOT FOR **YOU** TO DECIDE! **I** AM THE GOVERNOR. I MAKE THE LAWS. I CAN HAVE YOU **EXECUTED** FOR WHAT YOU'VE DONE.
BUT I AM NOT AN UNFAIR MAN.
I HEAR THAT YOU ARE QUITE THE **BOWMAN**, TELL.
SO PEOPLE SAY.
HE'S THE BEST BOWMAN IN THE CANTONS! WHY, HE CAN HIT A CHAMOIS THROUGH THE HEART AT A HUNDRED PACES. HE CAN BRING DOWN A RABBIT WHILE IT'S RUNNING.
WHO IS **THIS**, TELL?

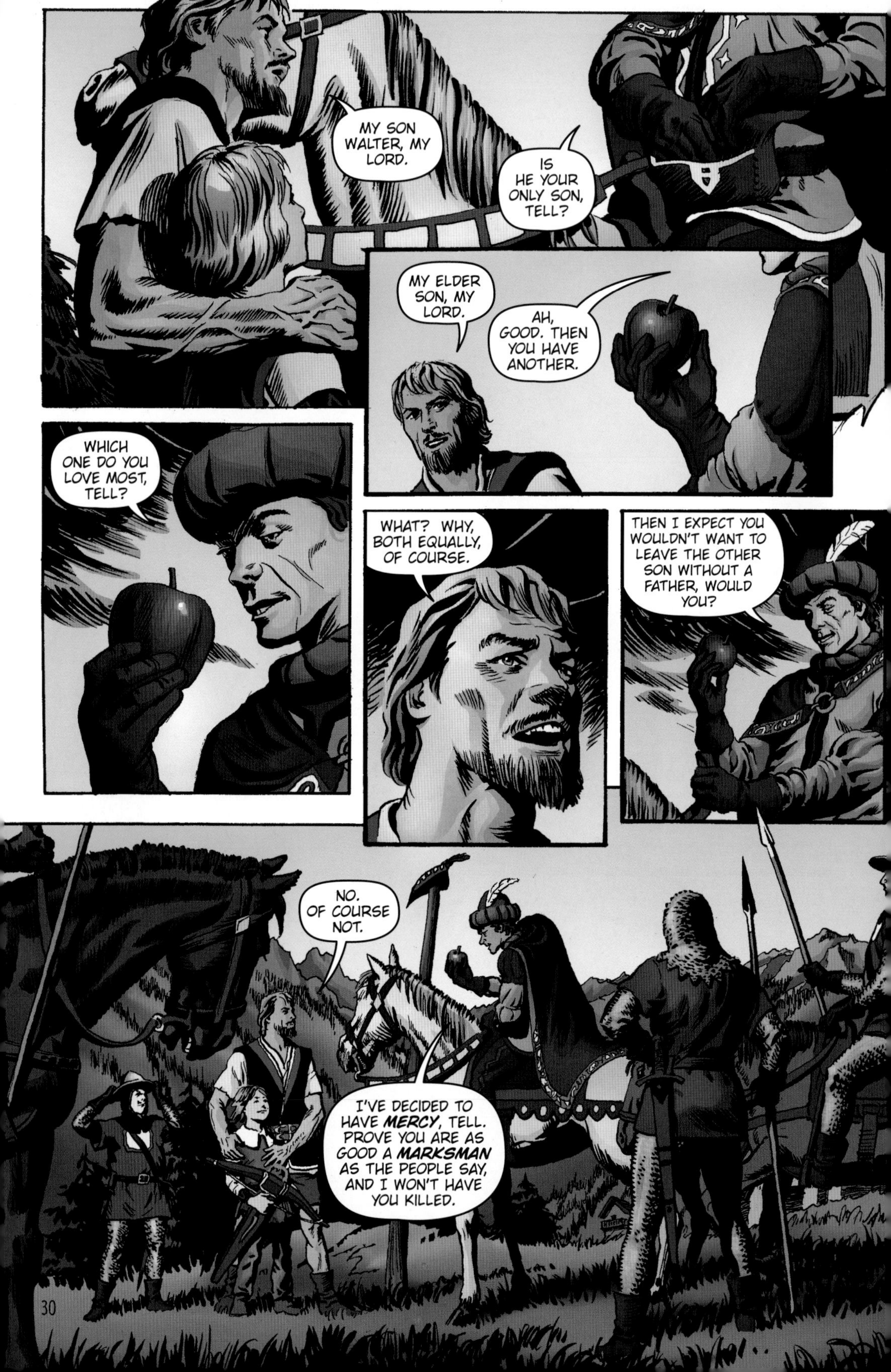
MY SON WALTER, MY LORD.
IS HE YOUR ONLY SON, TELL?
MY ELDER SON, MY LORD.
AH, GOOD. THEN YOU HAVE ANOTHER.
WHICH ONE DO YOU LOVE MOST, TELL?
WHAT? WHY, BOTH EQUALLY, OF COURSE.
THEN I EXPECT YOU WOULDN'T WANT TO LEAVE THE OTHER SON WITHOUT A FATHER, WOULD YOU?
NO. OF COURSE NOT.
I'VE DECIDED TO HAVE MERCY, TELL. PROVE YOU ARE AS GOOD A MARKSMAN AS THE PEOPLE SAY, AND I WON'T HAVE YOU KILLED.

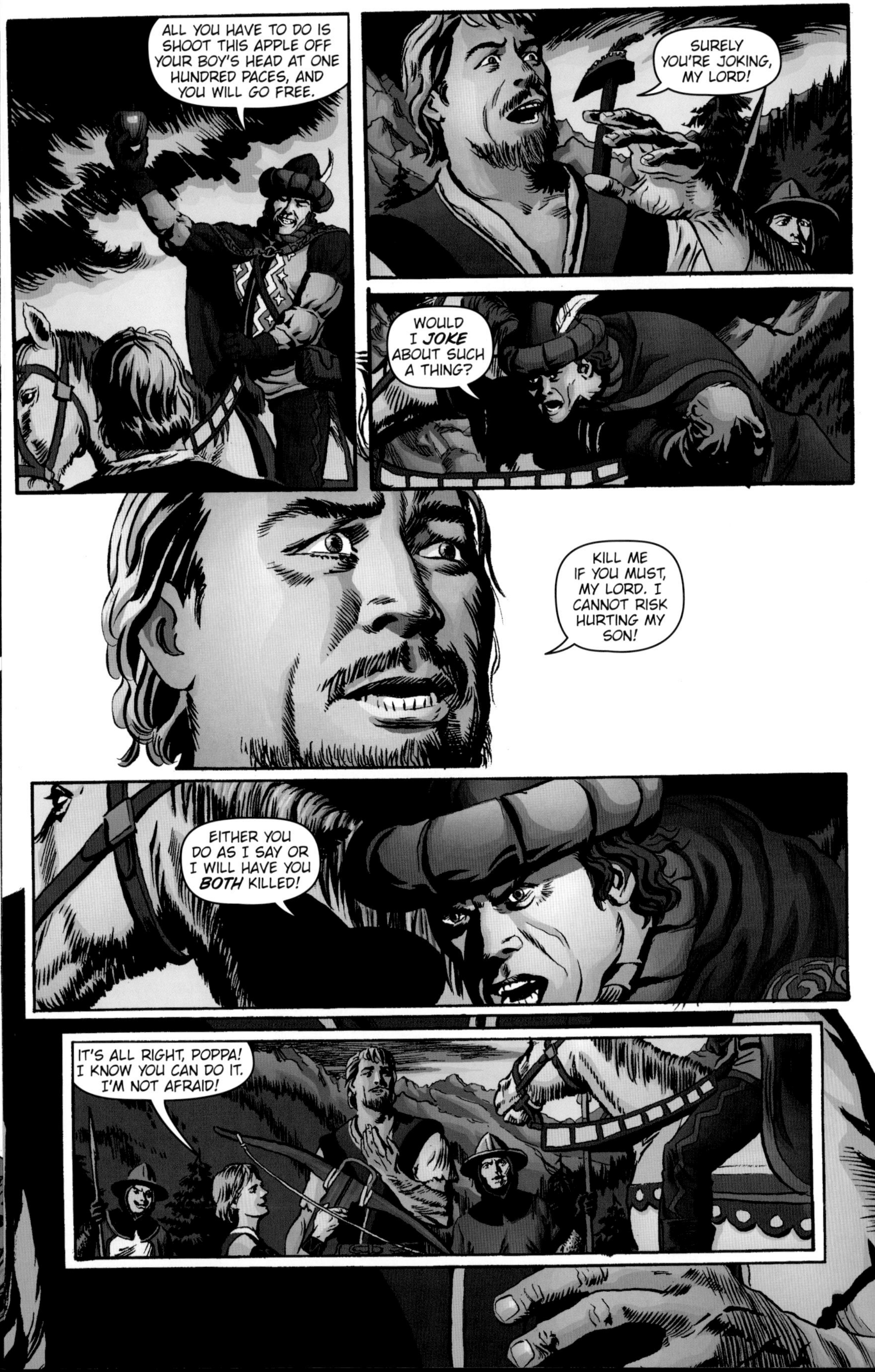
ALL YOU HAVE TO DO IS SHOOT THIS APPLE OFF YOUR BOY'S HEAD AT ONE HUNDRED PACES, AND YOU WILL GO FREE.
SURELY YOU'RE JOKING, MY LORD!
WOULD I JOKE ABOUT SUCH A THING?
KILL ME IF YOU MUST, MY LORD. I CANNOT RISK HURTING MY SON!
EITHER YOU DO AS I SAY OR I WILL HAVE YOU BOTH KILLED!
IT'S ALL RIGHT, POPPA! I KNOW YOU CAN DO IT. I'M NOT AFRAID!

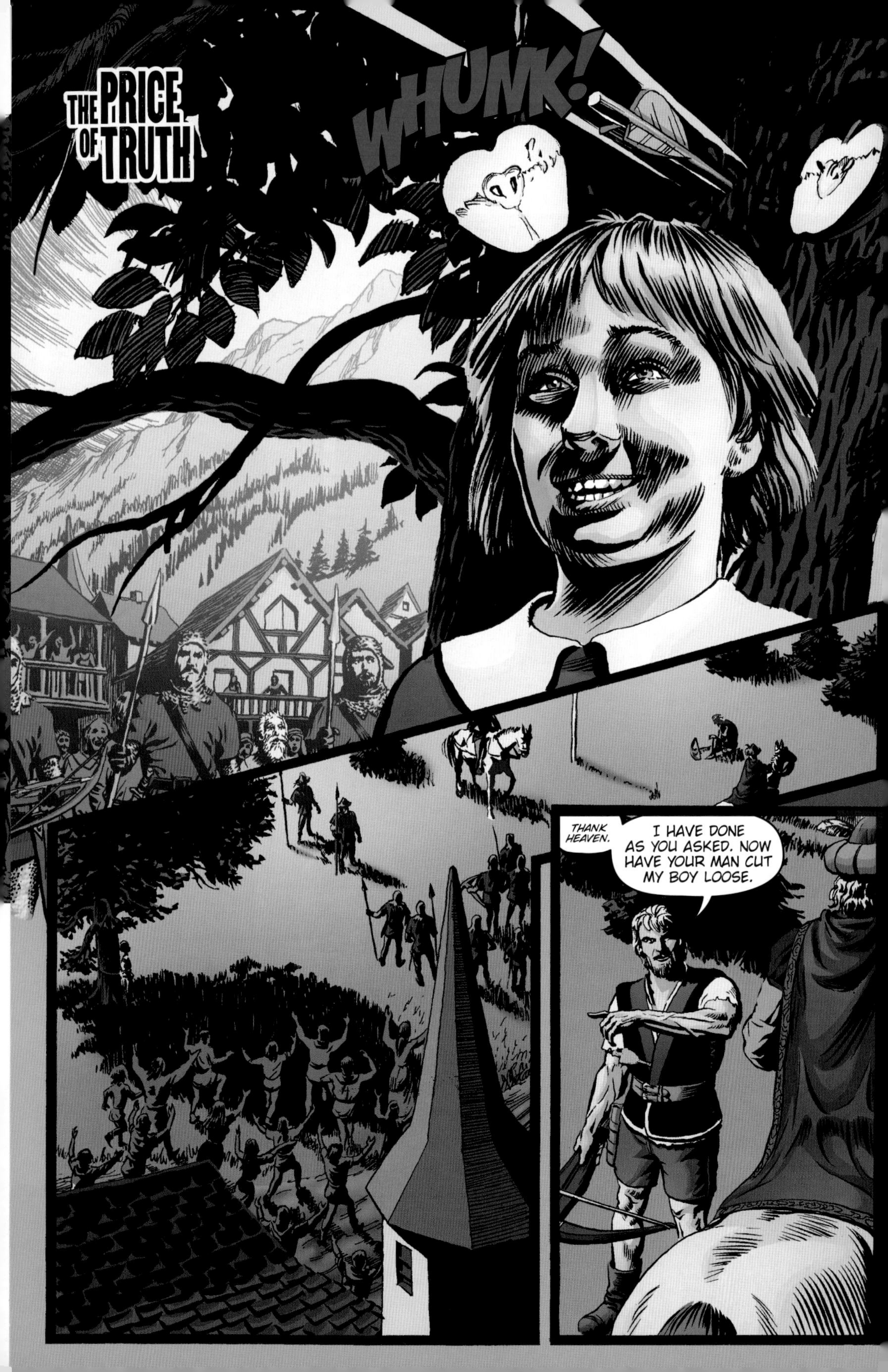
THE PRICE OF TRUTH
WHUNK!
THANK HEAVEN.
I HAVE DONE AS YOU ASKED. NOW HAVE YOUR MAN CUT MY BOY LOOSE.

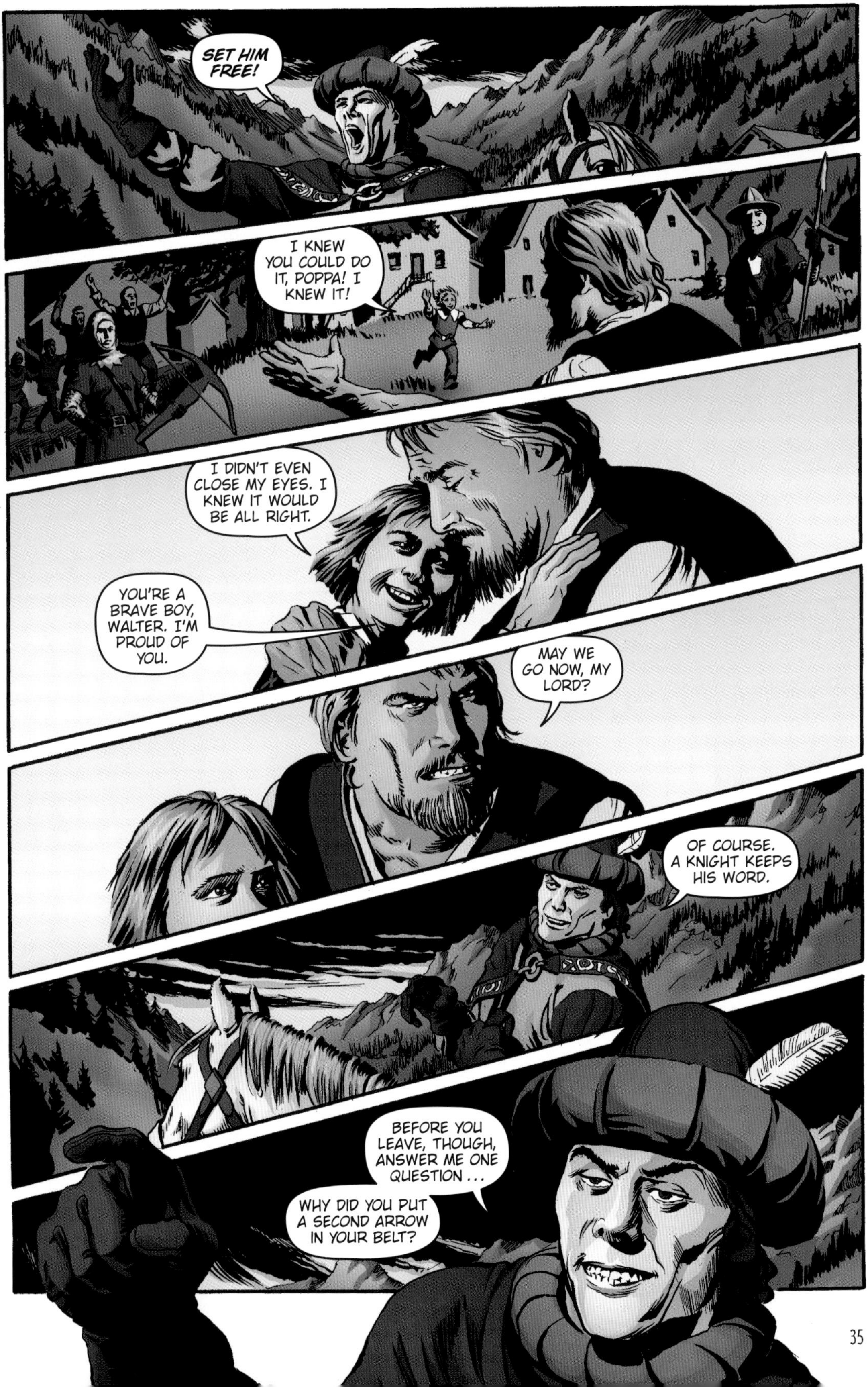
SET HIM FREE!
I KNEW YOU COULD DO IT, POPPA! I KNEW IT!
I DIDN'T EVEN CLOSE MY EYES. I KNEW IT WOULD BE ALL RIGHT.
YOU'RE A BRAVE BOY, WALTER. I'M PROUD OF YOU.
MAY WE GO NOW, MY LORD?
OF COURSE. A KNIGHT KEEPS HIS WORD.
BEFORE YOU LEAVE, THOUGH, ANSWER ME ONE QUESTION . . .
WHY DID YOU PUT A SECOND ARROW IN YOUR BELT?

IT'S AN OLD HUNTER'S CUSTOM, MY LORD. ALWAYS GOOD TO HAVE ANOTHER ARROW READY.

I DON'T BELIEVE YOU. COME NOW. TELL ME THE TRUTH. I PROMISE THAT YOUR LIFE IS IN NO DANGER.

WELL, THEN, THE TRUTH IS THE SECOND ARROW WAS FOR YOU.

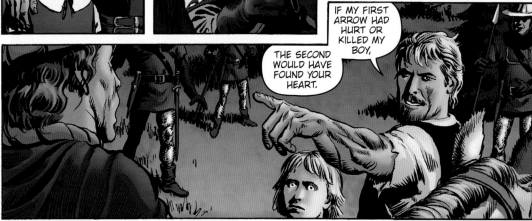

IF MY FIRST ARROW HAD HURT OR KILLED MY BOY,

THE SECOND WOULD HAVE FOUND YOUR HEART.

I THOUGHT SO! YOU ADMIT TO PLANNING TO KILL ME! ARREST THIS MAN!

LIAR! YOU GAVE YOUR WORD I WOULD GO FREE!

36

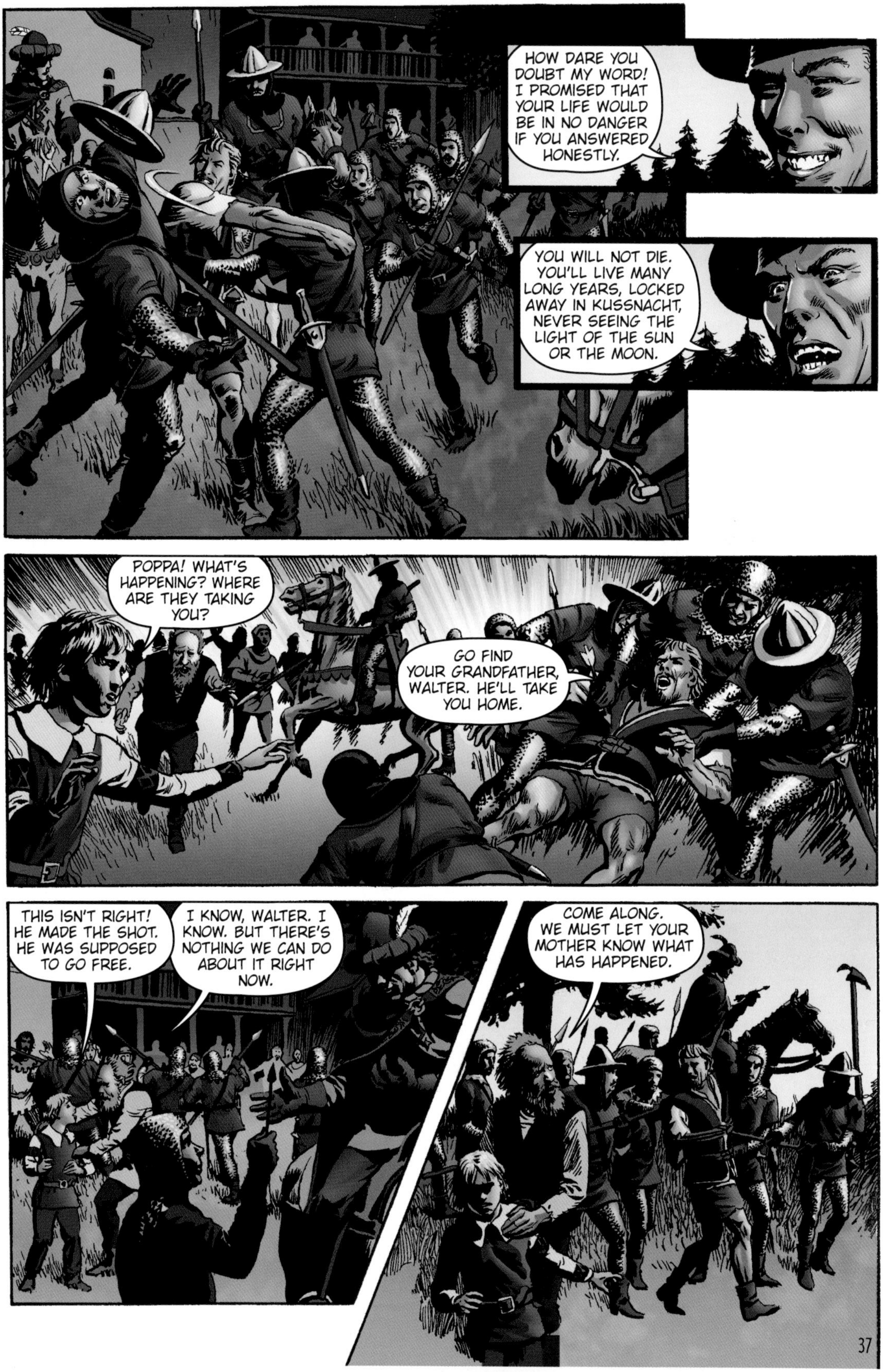

HOW DARE YOU DOUBT MY WORD! I PROMISED THAT YOUR LIFE WOULD BE IN NO DANGER IF YOU ANSWERED HONESTLY.
YOU WILL NOT DIE. YOU'LL LIVE MANY LONG YEARS, LOCKED AWAY IN KUSSNACHT, NEVER SEEING THE LIGHT OF THE SUN OR THE MOON.
POPPA! WHAT'S HAPPENING? WHERE ARE THEY TAKING YOU?
GO FIND YOUR GRANDFATHER, WALTER. HE'LL TAKE YOU HOME.
THIS ISN'T RIGHT! HE MADE THE SHOT. HE WAS SUPPOSED TO GO FREE.
I KNOW, WALTER. I KNOW. BUT THERE'S NOTHING WE CAN DO ABOUT IT RIGHT NOW.
COME ALONG. WE MUST LET YOUR MOTHER KNOW WHAT HAS HAPPENED.

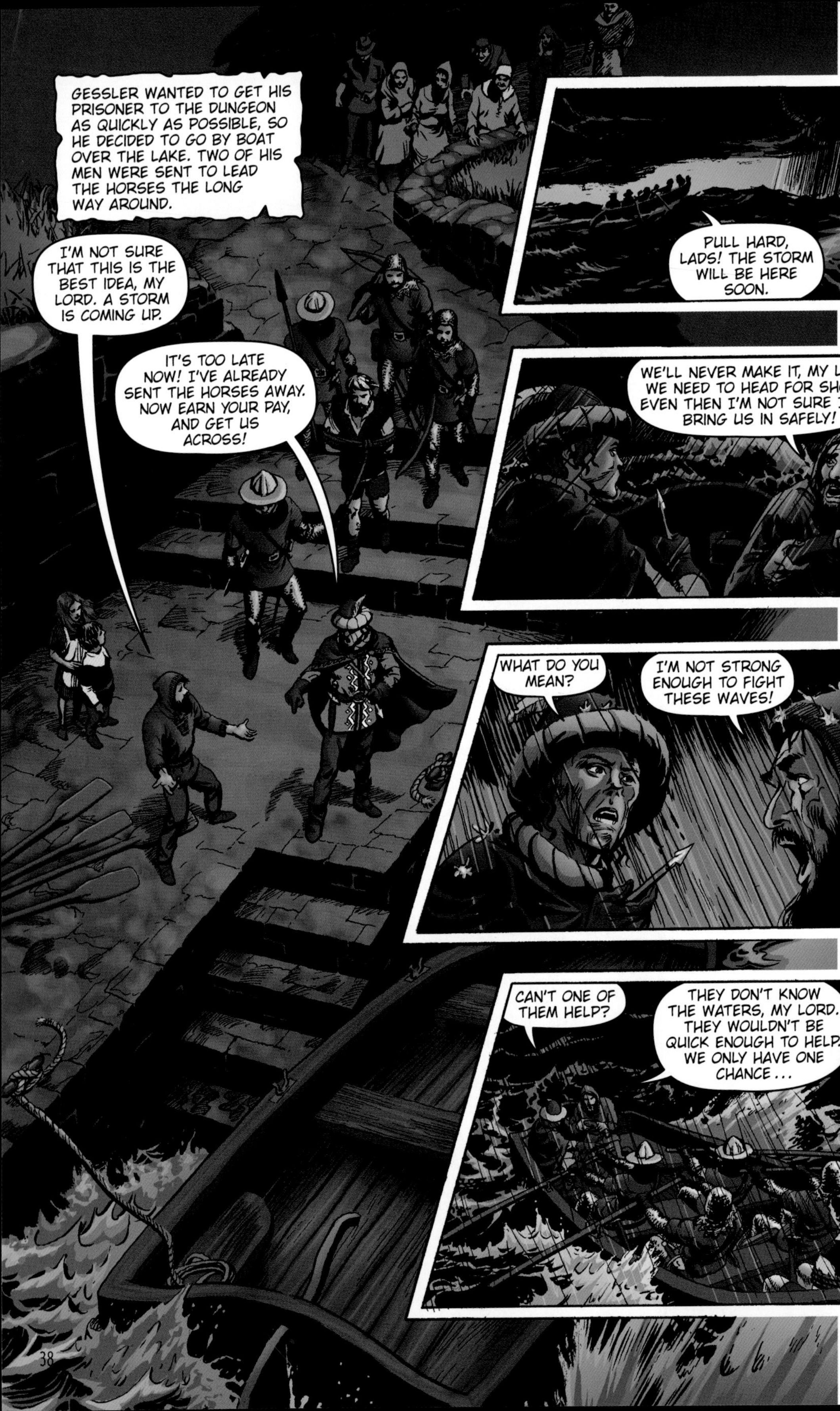
GESSLER WANTED TO GET HIS PRISONER TO THE DUNGEON AS QUICKLY AS POSSIBLE, SO HE DECIDED TO GO BY BOAT OVER THE LAKE. TWO OF HIS MEN WERE SENT TO LEAD THE HORSES THE LONG WAY AROUND.
I'M NOT SURE THAT THIS IS THE BEST IDEA, MY LORD. A STORM IS COMING UP.
IT'S TOO LATE NOW! I'VE ALREADY SENT THE HORSES AWAY. NOW EARN YOUR PAY, AND GET US ACROSS!
PULL HARD, LADS! THE STORM WILL BE HERE SOON.
WE'LL NEVER MAKE IT, MY LORD! WE NEED TO HEAD FOR SHORE. EVEN THEN I'M NOT SURE I CAN BRING US IN SAFELY!
WHAT DO YOU MEAN?
I'M NOT STRONG ENOUGH TO FIGHT THESE WAVES!
CAN'T ONE OF THEM HELP?
THEY DON'T KNOW THE WATERS, MY LORD. THEY WOULDN'T BE QUICK ENOUGH TO HELP. WE ONLY HAVE ONE CHANCE . . .

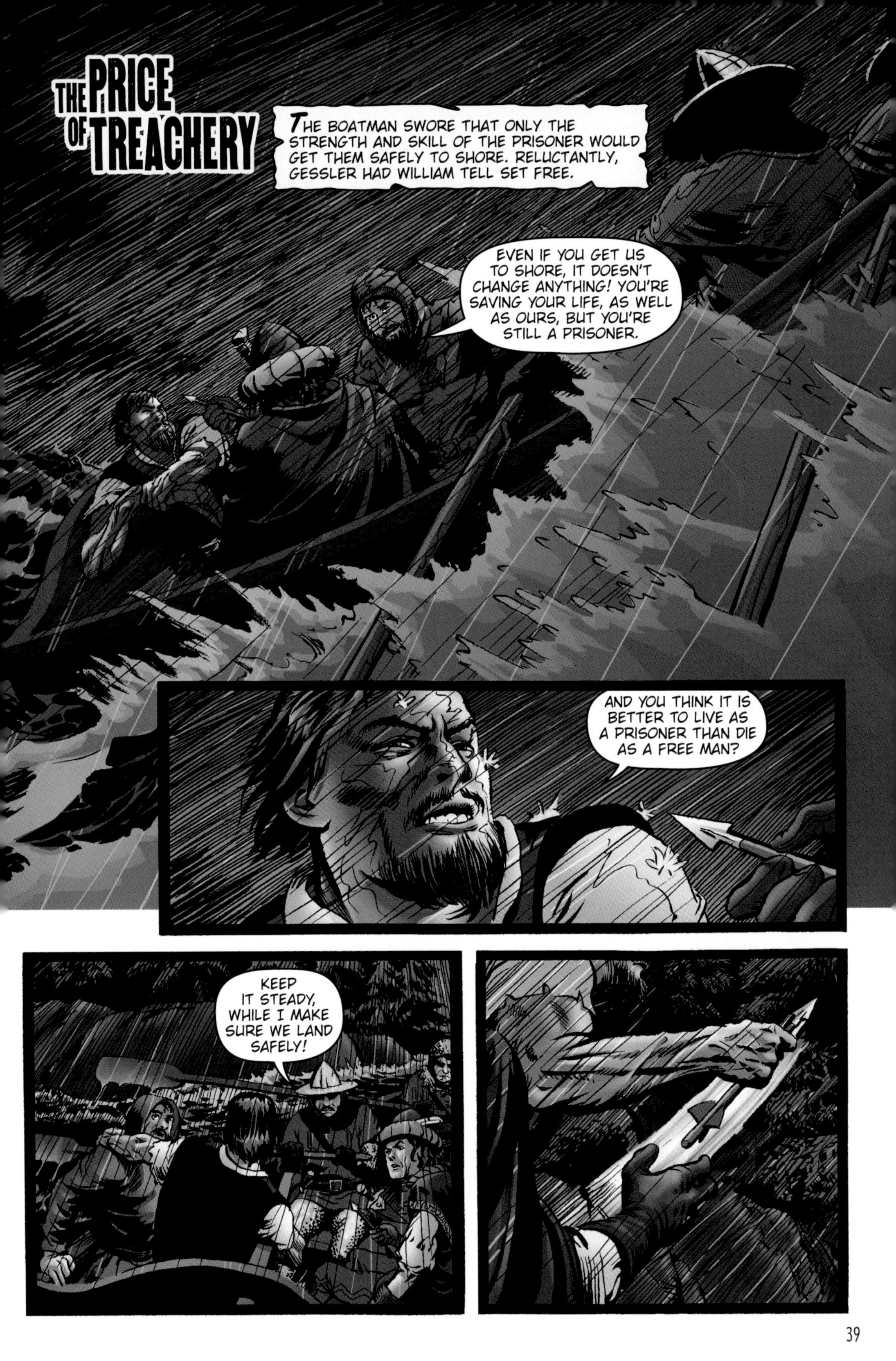
THE PRICE OF TREACHERY
THE BOATMAN SWORE THAT ONLY THE STRENGTH AND SKILL OF THE PRISONER WOULD GET THEM SAFELY TO SHORE. RELUCTANTLY, GESSLER HAD WILLIAM TELL SET FREE.
EVEN IF YOU GET US TO SHORE, IT DOESN'T CHANGE ANYTHING! YOU'RE SAVING YOUR LIFE, AS WELL AS OURS, BUT YOU'RE STILL A PRISONER.
AND YOU THINK IT IS BETTER TO LIVE AS A PRISONER THAN DIE AS A FREE MAN?
KEEP IT STEADY, WHILE I MAKE SURE WE LAND SAFELY!

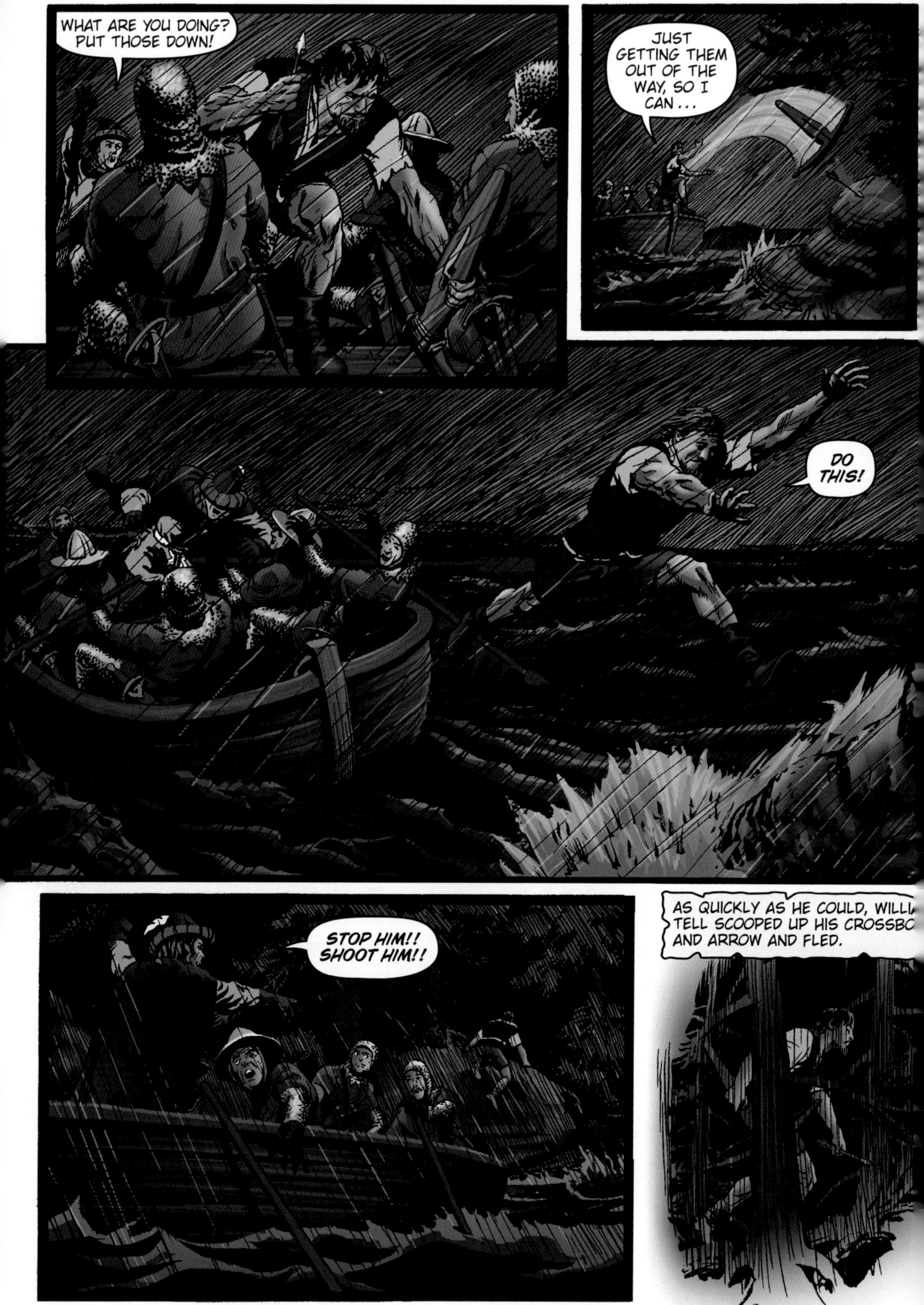
WHAT ARE YOU DOING? PUT THOSE DOWN!
JUST GETTING THEM OUT OF THE WAY, SO I CAN . . .
DO THIS!
STOP HIM!! SHOOT HIM!!
AS QUICKLY AS HE COULD, WILLI TELL SCOOPED UP HIS CROSSBO AND ARROW AND FLED.

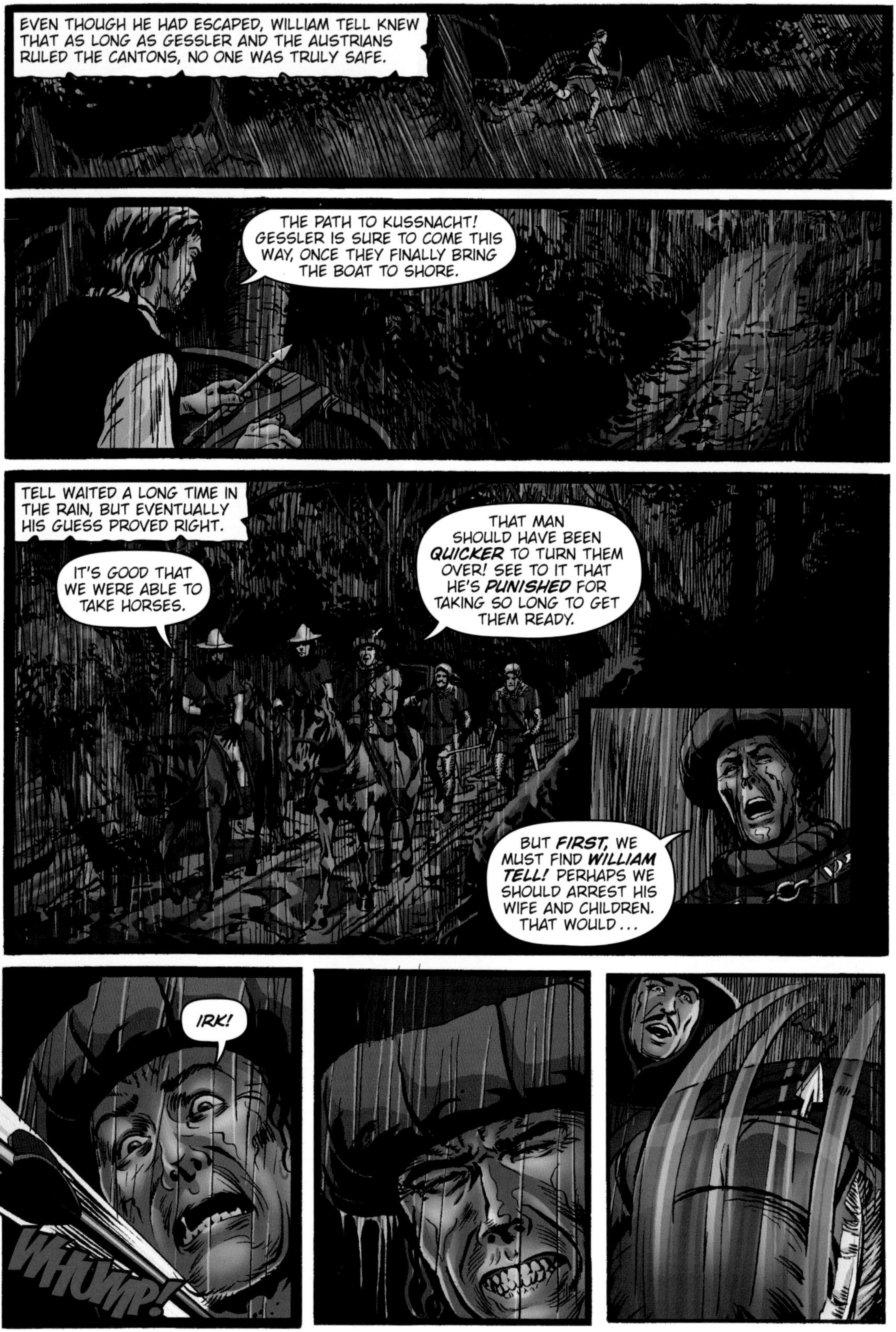
EVEN THOUGH HE HAD ESCAPED, WILLIAM TELL KNEW THAT AS LONG AS GESSLER AND THE AUSTRIANS RULED THE CANTONS, NO ONE WAS TRULY SAFE.
THE PATH TO KUSSNACHT! GESSLER IS SURE TO COME THIS WAY, ONCE THEY FINALLY BRING THE BOAT TO SHORE.
TELL WAITED A LONG TIME IN THE RAIN, BUT EVENTUALLY HIS GUESS PROVED RIGHT.
IT'S GOOD THAT WE WERE ABLE TO TAKE HORSES.
THAT MAN SHOULD HAVE BEEN QUICKER TO TURN THEM OVER! SEE TO IT THAT HE'S PUNISHED FOR TAKING SO LONG TO GET THEM READY.
BUT FIRST, WE MUST FIND WILLIAM TELL! PERHAPS WE SHOULD ARREST HIS WIFE AND CHILDREN. THAT WOULD . . .
IRK!
WHUMP!

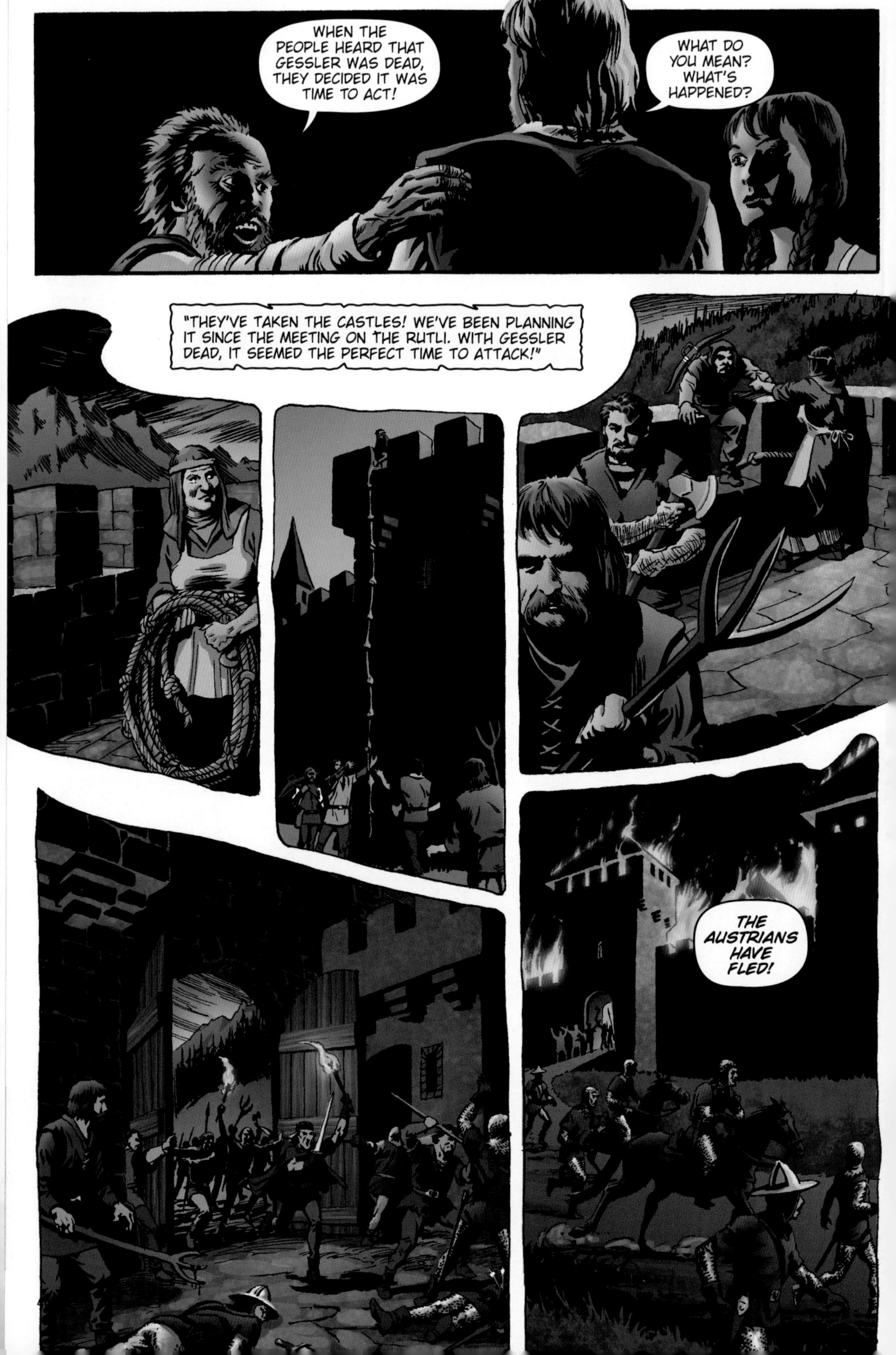
WHEN THE PEOPLE HEARD THAT GESSLER WAS DEAD, THEY DECIDED IT WAS TIME TO ACT!
WHAT DO YOU MEAN? WHAT'S HAPPENED?
"THEY'VE TAKEN THE CASTLES! WE'VE BEEN PLANNING IT SINCE THE MEETING ON THE RUTLI. WITH GESSLER DEAD, IT SEEMED THE PERFECT TIME TO ATTACK!"
THE AUSTRIANS HAVE FLED!

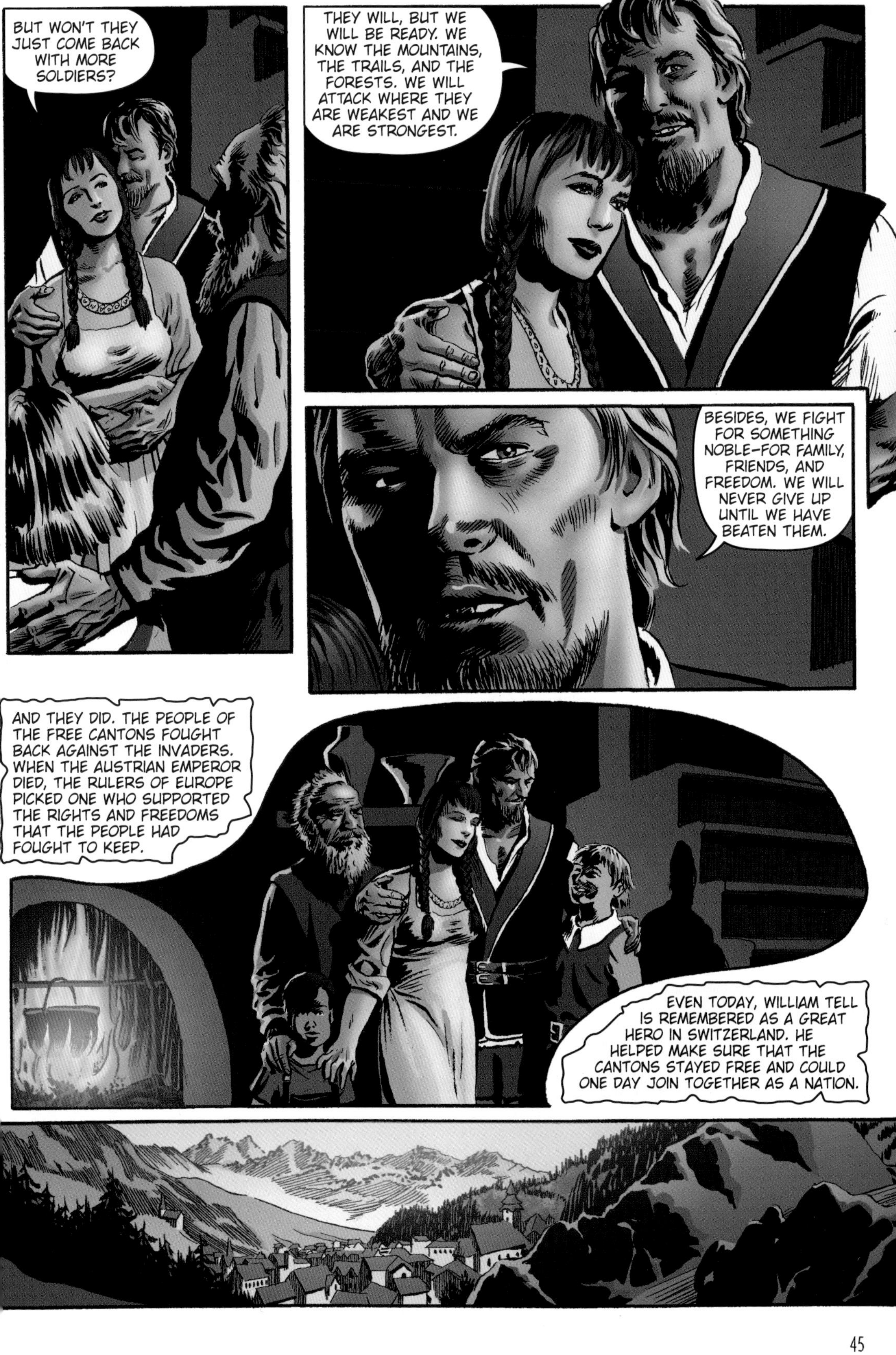
BUT WON'T THEY JUST COME BACK WITH MORE SOLDIERS?
THEY WILL, BUT WE WILL BE READY. WE KNOW THE MOUNTAINS, THE TRAILS, AND THE FORESTS. WE WILL ATTACK WHERE THEY ARE WEAKEST AND WE ARE STRONGEST.
BESIDES, WE FIGHT FOR SOMETHING NOBLE—FOR FAMILY, FRIENDS, AND FREEDOM. WE WILL NEVER GIVE UP UNTIL WE HAVE BEATEN THEM.
AND THEY DID. THE PEOPLE OF THE FREE CANTONS FOUGHT BACK AGAINST THE INVADERS. WHEN THE AUSTRIAN EMPEROR DIED, THE RULERS OF EUROPE PICKED ONE WHO SUPPORTED THE RIGHTS AND FREEDOMS THAT THE PEOPLE HAD FOUGHT TO KEEP.
EVEN TODAY, WILLIAM TELL IS REMEMBERED AS A GREAT HERO IN SWITZERLAND. HE HELPED MAKE SURE THAT THE CANTONS STAYED FREE AND COULD ONE DAY JOIN TOGETHER AS A NATION.

GLOSSARY AND PRONUNCIATION GUIDE

ALPS: a mountain range in Europe that passes through modern-day Switzerland

ARCHER: a person who uses a bow and arrow or crossbow

CANTON: a small territorial division of a land or country

CHAMOIS: a small, goatlike animal found in mountainous regions of Europe

CROSSBOW: a bow-and-arrow weapon that is mounted on a wooden stock

HOLY ROMAN EMPIRE: an empire of loosely joined states that covered much of modern-day Germany, Austria, and Italy. The Holy Roman Empire existed from the 9th or 10th century to 1806.

KEEP: fortress, castle

SENESCHAL: an agent or steward in charge of a lord's estate

TYRANNY: oppressive, brutal power

original pencil sketch from page 30

FURTHER READING AND WEBSITES

History of Switzerland: The Legend of William Tell
http://history-switzerland.geschichte-schweiz.ch/william-tell-switzerland-hero.html
    This site explores the legend of William Tell, his place in Swiss history,
and the many retellings of his story over the centuries. It also includes
images of classic works of art that feature William Tell.

Music with Ease: William Tell
http://www.musicwithease.com/william-tell-synopsis.html
    The legend of William Tell has been told in books, stories, plays—even an
opera. Visit this website to read a summary of the opera *William Tell*, which
was composed by Gioacchino Antonio Rossini and first performed in 1829.

Schiller, Friedrich. *Wilhelm Tell*.
    Chicago: University of Chicago Press, 1973. This is an English translation
from the German of Friedrich Schiller's famous 1804 play.

Storrie, Paul D. *Robin Hood: Outlaw of Sherwood Forest*.
    Minneapolis: Graphic Universe, 2007. The legend of another medieval hero,
Robin Hood in England, is brought to life in this graphic novel by author
Paul D. Storrie and artist Thomas Yeates.

William Tell Overture, Part 2
http://www.archive.org/details/EDIS-SRP-0197-05
    The opera *William Tell* features some very famous music that you may have
heard before. Visit this site to listen to a recording of some of the opera.

CREATING *WILLIAM TELL: ONE AGAINST AN EMPIRE*

To create this graphic novel adaptation, author Paul D. Storrie relied heavily
on classic retellings of the legend, including the play *Wilhelm Tell* (1804) by the
great German writer Friedrich Schiller and British writer P. G. Wodehouse's
William Tell Told Again (1904). To create a realistic setting for this book,
artist Thomas Yeates studied photographs of the scenery around Lake Lucerne
in Switzerland and referenced both medieval and modern works to ensure the
accuracy of the characters' dress.

INDEX

ABOUT THE AUTHOR AND THE ARTIST

PAUL D. STORRIE was born and raised in Detroit, Michigan, and has returned to live there again and again after living in other cities and states. He began writing professionally in 1998 and has written comics for Caliber Comics, Moonstone Books, Bluewater Productions, Marvel Comics, and DC Comics. Some of the titles he's worked on include *Batman Beyond*, *Gotham Girls*, *Justice League Unlimited* and *Captain America: Red, White & Blue*. His many Graphic Universe™ titles include *Hercules: The Twelve Labors*, *Amaterasu: Return of the Sun*, *Yu the Great: Conquering the Flood*, *Robin Hood: Outlaw of Sherwood*, *Perseus: The Hunt for Medusa's Head*, and *Beowulf: Monster Slayer* from the Graphic Myths and Legends series. He also wrote *Terror in Ghost Mansion* for the Graphic Universe Twisted Journeys™ series.

THOMAS YEATES began his art training in high school and continued at Utah State University and Sacramento State University. Subsequently, he was a member of the first class at Joe Kubert's School, a trade program for aspiring comic-book artists in New Jersey. Yeates has worked as an illustrator for DC Comics, Marvel, Dark Horse, and many other companies, drawing *Tarzan*, *Zorro*, *The Swamp Thing*, *Time Spirits*, *Captain America*, and *Conan*. Yeates's many titles for the Graphic Myths and Legends series include *King Arthur: Excalibur Unsheathed*, *Arthur & Lancelot: The Fight for Camelot*, *Atalanta: The Race against Destiny*, *Robin Hood: Outlaw of Sherwood Forest*, *Odysseus: Escaping Poseidon's Curse*, and *Perseus: The Hunt for Medusa's Head*.